# Sea Island Yankee

# Sea Island Yankee

*by Clyde Bresee*

*With illustrations by Paul M. Williams*

University of South Carolina Press

Map by Anna E. Birkner

First published 1986 by Algonquin Books of Chapel Hill

First paperback edition 1995
Published in Columbia, South Carolina, by the
University of South Carolina Press

Manufactured in the United States of America

99  98  97  96  95      5  4  3  2  1

### Library of Congress Cataloging-in-Publication Data

Bresee, Clyde, 1916–
     Sea Island Yankee / by Clyde Bresee : with illustrations by Paul
M  Williams. —1st paperback ed.
        p.   cm
     ISBN 1–57003–095–2
     1. Bresee, Clyde, 1916–    . 2. James Island (S.C.)—Biography.
3. James Island (S.C.)—Social life and customs. 4. Sea Islands—
Biography. 5. Sea Islands—Social life and customs. I. Title
[F277.B3B743     1995]
813'.54—dc20                                          95–32653

For my wife, Elizabeth,
and for my children, Jerome and Catherine

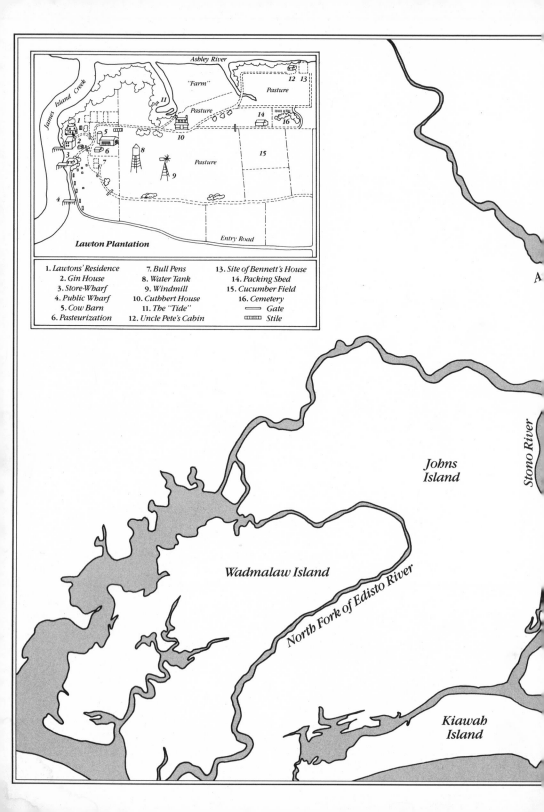

**Lawton Plantation**

1. Lawtons' Residence
2. Gin House
3. Store-Wharf
4. Public Wharf
5. Cow Barn
6. Pasteurization
7. Bull Pens
8. Water Tank
9. Windmill
10. Cuthbert House
11. The "Tide"
12. Uncle Pete's Cabin
13. Site of Bennett's House
14. Packing Shed
15. Cucumber Field
16. Cemetery
Gate
Stile

Ashley River
"Farm"
Pasture
Pasture
Pasture
James Island Creek
Entry Road

Johns Island
Wadmalaw Island
Stono River
North Fork of Edisto River
Kiawah Island

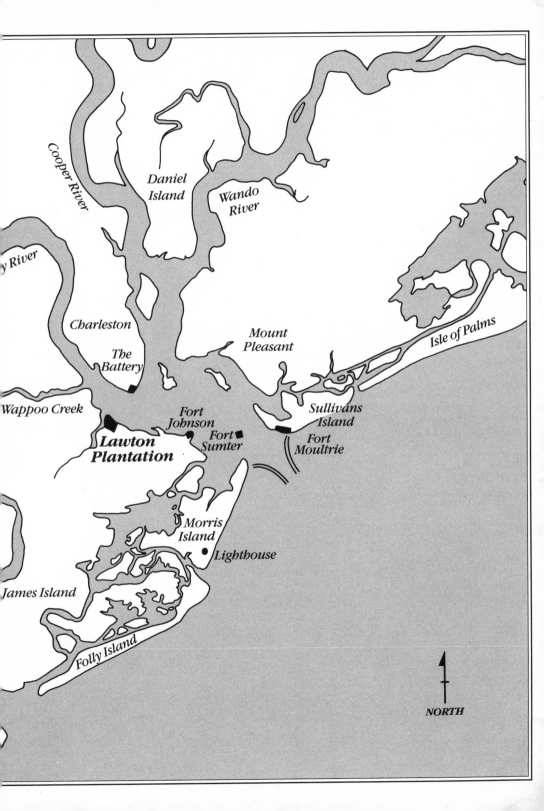

# Contents

# Contents

# Sea Island Yankee

# *I*

# *Two Live Oaks*

As my mother tells it, the letter came to our little Pennsylvania farm in the fall of 1919.

"St. John Alison Lawton, Charleston, South Carolina," she read on the envelope as she walked from the mailbox toward the house. The letter was addressed to my father. "But who is St. John Alison Lawton?" she mused. "What an odd name . . . St. John Alison . . . Plantation, James Island . . . We don't know any Lawtons or anybody in South Carolina."

She put the letter on the shelf in front of the clock. My father would explain when he came in from the field. I was only four years old when this letter arrived and, of course, knew nothing of it then. I sensed only the changes that began to occur in our lives—changes that would take me from a little dairy farm in northern Pennsylvania to a Sea Island near Charleston, South Carolina—one of the most historic islands along that historic coastline. From a family-operated farm, where my mother had taken her babies to the barn in the morning to help her husband with the milking, I would be transported to a culture of plantation owners living in the afterglow of a landed aristocracy. We would meet for the first time a subculture of Negro workers who performed nearly all the manual labor on a plantation, and who were in a state of semiservitude to their white employers. I would go from a climate whose ninety-day growing season drove farmers to almost frantic activity as they prepared for the frosts of September, to one of a long summer that drifted into a long hazy autumn, followed by a brief winter—daffodils and violets in February, and the blaze of azaleas in March. There would be people of gentler manners than I had known; people of intense loyalties born of a past that had been violently wrenched from them. There would be a life dominated by the sea, a coastal city by an ever-changing harbor, the wandering tidal streams, and the vast mystery of the marshes.

The letter that my mother placed in front of the clock that fall day was as much a surprise to my father as it was to her. His "explanation" set in motion a chain of events that neither of them could have then anticipated. Two weeks earlier my father had read an advertisement in the *Holstein Friesian World* for a herdsman to manage a large dairy plantation on James Island near Charleston, South Carolina. "I answered the ad late one night," he is supposed to have said, "mostly out of curiosity."

The letter he received from St. John Alison Lawton began: "My farm is situated one and a half miles across the Ashley River from Charleston, to which place my milk is taken by launch twice a day. By road the distance is about eight miles. My plantation has been used by me years past as a cotton and truck plantation—with a dairy farm. Owing to the boll weevil, the cotton will be abandoned, and because of the shortage of negro labor, we are moving out of the truck business."

My father apparently expressed a desire for more information, for there began immediately a lengthy exchange of letters. The other day as I was going through my father's papers, I found the letters written to him by St. John Alison Lawton, neatly tied in a bundle and tucked far back in the roll-top desk. The formal stationery was headed:

> St. John Alison Lawton
> Holstein Friesian Cattle

Plantation, James Island
41 South Bay
Charleston, S.C.

The story begins, who knows how many years earlier, with a sense of restlessness and perhaps of futility that began to grow in my father. The round of milking, plowing, and haying on a fertile, tiny Pennsylvania farm that was hedged in by lands of his father-in-law and brother-in-law failed to satisfy him. There had been a mortgage, three children within four years, an uncertain market for his product, and almost no opportunity to apply the principles of dairy husbandry that he had learned in college. Ever a romantic, he had envisioned a family farm of fine cattle, strong, gentle horses, and a flock of cheerful hens from which he might gather eggs at sundown. It hadn't quite worked out. Comments dropped by my relatives years later caused me to think he wanted to escape from what he considered to be the smothering presence of my mother's strongly religious family. Rectitude and participation in what Methodists called "the means of grace" were expected of all in that extended family. Rectitude did not trouble my father, but conformity—or an adequate explanation for his nonconformity—to a sequence of morning services, evening services, Bible studies, prayer meetings, class meetings, love feasts, and the annual revival meeting probably did trouble him. No one ever told me—if anyone, including perhaps himself, knew—exactly what stirrings impelled him late one night to inquire about a position in far-off South Carolina.

On January 25, 1920, Alison Lawton wrote inviting my father to come down and "try things out for a while and see for yourself the prospects and difficulties." He went on to state that he believed a good living could be made on the plantation and that "in ten years you will find yourself worth more than where you are."

Another letter in the spring of that year described the loss of several cows from hemorrhagic septicemia and the cost of inoculating the herd. Mr. Lawton was apparently trying to present a true picture of the economic aspects of the plantation because he reported planting a large crop of peanuts when the price was $220 a ton, and of a market collapse just before harvest time that lowered the price to $55 a ton. He decided to feed the peanuts to the cows rather than to sell so cheaply.

To my father's inquiry about malaria, Alison Lawton replied that there had been no case of the disease among the whites on the island for years. "I will acknowledge that the Negroes sometimes have it; but they roam all around, don't screen their houses and don't take any precautions."

For a few months, correspondence seemed to have lagged; then Alison Lawton wrote again: "I have often thought of the correspondence with you, and somehow out of the 70-odd replies to my 'ad,' I have often imagined you were the man I wanted to tie up to."

In response to this letter, my father did go for a two-week inspection trip. Then this letter from Mr. Lawton: "Have you changed your mind yet? Don't you think you might consider fixing up the old house by those live oaks? I'm sure that is a beautiful location and could be fixed up if you could come some time this fall."

He then outlined the financial arrangements he would offer. My father and he would each draw $150 per month for living expenses, with one-fourth of the monthly balance to go to each. The remainder of the profit would be divided according to the financial interest of each.

I believe this is a good proposition and would lead to your being owner of this valuable property that has supported my grandfather, my father, and myself for over 100 years. This is an opportunity for a hard-working man, who has some brains, for a comfortable living that he can put up money for his old age and for his children.

The view from our place of the city across the water is magnificent and the climate is not bad.

My father apparently then asked about race relations on the island, to which Mr. Lawton replied that "as fine and honest and refined people have grown up on these Sea Islands as you will find anywhere in the country. Because the white people observe strict honesty, the negroes respect and trust them."

The last letter contains this bit of enticement:

This plantation has provided a good living since 1813 for three men— myself, my father, and my grandfather. With its excellent location—one mile from Charleston—and pastures judged to be some of the finest in the state, we should be able to make money.

The Cuthbert house where I lived as a boy is in need of repairs which I shall make, but I think you will like its location with two large live oaks in the yard and the view of the city.

St. John Alison Lawton had painted a picture of his Sea Island plantation that was at once attractive and forbidding. The attractions won and our little family went to live on the Lawton plantation in the house by the two live oaks.

Our train inched backward into the Charleston peninsula, joggling over noisy switches, edging its way past the corners of long, gray warehouses, testing our patience to the limit, until it stopped at last in Union Station. It was the day before Thanksgiving, 1921.

The aisle of the Pullman car quickly filled with a procession of passengers eager to leave, but unable to move. My mother decided not to risk her brood of three children in the crowd; she sat down to wait. I returned to the window and pressed my face against the glass looking in the crowd on the station platform for my father who had come three weeks earlier. Suddenly our eyes met and we waved. He spoke to a dignified-looking man at his side who also waved. I was sure he was the man who owned the big plantation where we were going to live. I waved until I heard my mother's impatient voice calling me.

Bundled in our warm Pennsylvania clothes, Gladys, Kenneth, and I led the way off the train. We descended into a cloud of steam that was pouring from under the car, and waited for the conductor to help my mother with her suitcase. My father came up, gave us hugs all around, and told the Red Cap porter to take our luggage to the Columbus Street entrance. He then turned to introduce us to the smiling, gray-haired man beside him, Mr. St. John Alison Lawton. My mother was first. Mr. Lawton removed a soft, cream-colored hat, bowed, took my mother's hand and said he was "indeed happy" to meet her, and hoped she would like her new home in the South. He shook her hand for a long time. Then, to my surprise, he gravely shook hands with each of us children, speaking each of our names as he did so.

We joined the porter at Columbus Street in what seemed the sunshine of a warm summer's day. I felt hot and awkward in my winter overcoat. Mr. Lawton led us to a strange, box-shaped auto, which he called "the Anderson," and while the porter stored our luggage on the running board, Mr. Lawton opened the outside door of the car. Then he unlocked a little gate, located between the two front seats, that led into the rear compartment. My mother and we three children filed in, my father tipped the porter, took his place in the front beside Mr. Lawton, and the car began to move.

I did not know the street names then, but I am sure that we were soon driving down Spring Street. Crowded wooden houses with their gable ends pointing toward us—and black people everywhere. Up North, I had seen the only Negro in town when

I had visited my grandparents at the county seat; I had also watched the porters on the train. But I had never before seen sidewalks full of black people. Most amazing of all were the little black babies in their mothers' arms, and the children trailing them afoot. As we drove along, I tried to watch what everyone was doing on the sidewalk, and at the same time listen to the conversation in the car. I heard Mr. Lawton say that he would take us directly to James Island. "I could carry you down to the Battery and let you cross the Ashley River in my launch, but I think the boat will be loaded with freight this afternoon. We'll save that trip for another day."

My father seemed quite familiar with the route we were taking. "We're going to cross a long wooden bridge in a minute," he said. "Keep your eyes open because you may be able to see some big ships." He was right, for we were soon clattering across the old wooden bridge that spanned the Ashley River. It was the longest, noisiest bridge that I had ever ridden on. Through the railings we could see gray, choppy water on either side, looking like a lake to us who had known only the Susquehanna River cutting through the Pennsylvania mountains. My father was also right about the ships; we saw one that had two smokestacks and a big white deck on which people were walking. We could now see fields of brown marsh grass that seemed to stretch up and down the river for miles and far back to a line of trees.

The Anderson was moving cautiously over the noisy boards toward the marsh, when suddenly the clattering stopped. Our wheels had moved onto a packed-clay causeway. In a few minutes a second bridge over a smaller river, the same rattling boards, and then silence as our wheels hit soft sand. Mr. Lawton turned to us in the back seat and said a little grandly, "You are now on James Island."

Our road was soon lined with dense hedges, broken occasionally by open spaces that led to cabin dooryards.

"Being on an island, I had expected to see more water," my mother observed.

"Oh, there's water enough," my father said. "These rivers that we've been crossing make the islands. There are a lot of them around Charleston. And the Atlantic Ocean is over there," he added, pointing to the left. "If we cross a river off to our right, we'll be on John's Island."

Mr. Lawton now gave all his attention to guiding the car through heavy sand, so thick and deep that the old Anderson would lurch violently if the front wheels strayed from the rut. There was much that we wanted to tell our father: a train ride to New York City, our first night on a Pullman, and breakfast in the dining car, but he was busy pointing out landmarks.

"How long before we get to our house?" my sister asked.

"About a half hour," Mr. Lawton said. He turned to my mother. "We are going to take you to the other end of the island, Mrs. Bresee, right across the harbor from the Battery. I think you will like the location."

"Our furniture has arrived and it's all unpacked," my father announced.

The Anderson ground slowly along while we tried to look in all directions at once. We stared in fascination at the Negro people everywhere—everywhere. We rode at times through a tunnel of trees whose branches were hung with long, gray strands of Spanish moss moving sinuously in the breeze. Two days earlier we had boarded our train by a mountain that rose straight out of the Susquehanna River; here was flatness and sand, expanses of quiet water and marsh grass, and the mysterious moss over our heads. After we had plowed through the sand for about six miles, we turned into one of the field roads of the Lawton plantation. We followed a hedgerow for a while, then took a turn onto a little rise of ground that overlooked the plantation buildings. We stopped for a better view, as Mr. Lawton pointed to the stream that flowed into the harbor and to his fields and his barns.

"The largest building you see is the gin house," Mr. Lawton said, "but we no longer raise cotton. The gin house was built near the water so that cotton bales could easily be loaded into boats."

Somewhat back from the stream we could see the milking barns, a tile silo, and other low buildings. "This plantation was named 'The Bluff' many years ago because the land by the creek there and the place where my house stands are the highest points on James Island." I was to learn later that fifteen feet above sea level was high.

"I have nearly a mile of waterfront on the Ashley River," he said. He turned to the rear seat. "Can you children see the city over yonder?"

In the distance I could see the skyline of Charleston across a vast expanse of marsh that swept away to my left to a far-off border of trees. Over the marsh a dozen large black birds were slowly circling in a gently ascending spiral.

"We love this view of the city." Mr. Lawton was speaking again. "The two tall steeples that you see are St. Michael's and St. Philip's—two of our most historic churches. You'll learn about them after you have lived here awhile."

Mr. Lawton started up the car and we continued through a settlement of cabins around which women and children stood silently watching us. I remember thinking it strange that people lived in such little houses—open doorways with no screens and square holes in the walls for windows that could be covered only by a solid wooden blind. A woman with a pipe nodded deeply as we drove past, and Mr. Lawton nodded in return.

"They are some of our families," he said.

We drove past a lot where cattle were standing outside of long barns. There were Negro men everywhere. It was late afternoon and milking was in progress. Here at last was something that I had seen up North. We then followed a sandy road past dairy barns that led to a fair-sized house which Mr. Lawton said was his home. It was a two-storied wooden house built on high brick columns; a gently sloping roof, punctuated by two dormer windows, extended down over a broad front porch that was edged by a low banister railing. Two flights of steps led up to the porch— one at the front with a vine-covered arbor above it, and another at the end toward the river—giving the house a comfortable, welcoming look. The view over the river to the west across an endless expanse of marsh grass was like nothing I had ever seen before. Immediately in front of us was a stream that Mr. Lawton had called James Island Creek.

As we parked the car under the arbor in front of the house, Mrs. Lawton, a large woman with nearly white hair, came smiling down the steps and said, "Well, I'm mighty glad to see you." She shook hands all around and led us to chairs on the porch. Mr. Lawton and my father took seats a little to one side and discontinued their conversation, seeming to enjoy watching Mrs. Lawton preside. I liked her immediately.

"Mrs. Bresee, I know this is quite different from Pennsylvania. Did you have a pleasant trip?"

"Very pleasant," my mother replied. "But we are not used to so much flat country."

Then Mrs. Lawton said that she was born in Virginia, near Lynchburg, and when Mr. Lawton brought her to James Island she was terribly homesick for the rolling hills she had known. Then they talked about the low country and agreed that there was beauty here in the oaks, the Spanish moss, and the slow streams.

Mrs. Lawton then asked us children if we liked roast goose. She hoped we did because she had asked Flora, her cook, to roast one, and Ned had put it on our kitchen table. The goose came from a flock right here on the plantation.

While we talked, a peacock came around the corner of the house, emitted what I learned later was the typical peacock call, and spread his tail. As he edged cautiously toward us, he gave soft chucking sounds that sent little tremors across his big tail. "Bless you, Carlton," Mrs. Lawton said. "Now you're going to show off. How did you know we had guests from Pennsylvania?" She turned to my parents. "We've had a pair of peafowls on the plantation for as long as I can remember."

When Mr. Lawton and my father decided to walk down to the gin house for a few minutes, Mrs. Lawton took us over to the edge of the porch for a better view. Beyond the lawn was marsh grass, a bank of mud, and James Island Creek—a stream that she said flowed into the Ashley River. Plantation boats made trips twice a day out this creek carrying milk, freight, and mail to the city. Passengers could ride for a small fee because it was easier to reach Charleston by boat than to go around by the road. "Unless," she added, "we have a storm. Then our launches have trouble."

My mother said that in Pennsylvania we were bothered by thunderstorms and blizzards. There weren't any blizzards in South Carolina, but in the fall big hurricanes came up the coast and often did much damage. "The tide sometimes comes in to twice its usual height, but we feel safe here, because this is one of the highest places on James Island. The Cuthbert house where you will live is also on high ground."

I wanted to see one of the plantation boats, and I asked her when one would come. "Not until morning," she said, "after the milking is done."

The men returned from the gin house, and we walked over to the Anderson car. Again, Mr. Lawton opened the two doors and we filed into the back seat, waved good-bye, and then made our way for a quarter of a mile through pasture land, a grove of live oaks, and up a little grade to our new home—the Cuthbert house. Mr. Lawton escorted us to the door and told us to let him know if we needed any help. We waited on the porch and waved as he drove away.

Then a rush inside and to the kitchen and the roast goose. There it was in a big black roasting pan.

"This is certainly a lovely thing for Mrs. Lawton to do," my mother said as she lifted the cover. "Oh!" my mother said in an almost shocked voice. "I wonder . . ."—her voice broke off suddenly.

We stood in a circle looking at the goose. It was a little too brown, perhaps, but it gave off a delectable odor.

"What's the matter?" someone said.

"Nothing—nothing at all," my mother said.

My father came to the point. "I don't know who could put a goose in the oven with this many pin feathers in it."

"Flora did," my sister said. "She's Mrs. Lawton's cook."

"Well, they're really only bad on the wings—and we can cut them off," my father said.

Dear old Flora. We came to know her well and to love her, even though her standards for roasting a goose were not those of a Pennsylvania farm wife. My mother said later that Flora probably had poor eyesight. "Poor old thing," she said. "How could she afford to buy glasses on her wages?"

We children were hopping about the table talking about roasted pin feathers when my mother suddenly took command.

"You children come here. Now listen hard. This goose is a nice present for us and it will be perfectly all right. And don't one of you ever—do you hear me?—ever talk about these pin feathers to

anyone outside of this family. I would feel awful if you did. Do you understand?"

We swore eternal secrecy and ran back outdoors. Kenneth was calling to us from the front yard. "Look at that big swing!"

We rushed to join him. In front of the house were two immense trees whose gnarled, spreading branches made a kind of canopy over the yard. Their trunks, short and easily three feet in diameter, were covered with dark, deeply furrowed bark. Huge, bark-covered roots that seemed to have been forced out of the ground years ago sprawled around the base of the trees. We rushed to join Kenneth at the swing. We did not know it then, but we were playing in the shade of two historic live oaks—trees that were growing when Winfield Lawton, Alison's grandfather, acquired the plantation in 1813. We liked to think that these oaks had been planted in 1747, the year our house was built, but no one knew for certain.

## 2

# *By James Island Creek*

I was awakened that first morning on James Island by the sound of someone chopping wood. I rushed to the north window and saw in the backyard a two-wheeled cart hitched to a sleepy-looking mule who stood with one foot half raised. On the ground lay a pile of fresh pole wood that a Negro man was chopping into stove-length pieces. I would learn later that Ned, the yardman, had been told to have a pile of wood ready for the new family. Beyond the woodpile a ploughed field stretched back to blue water—the Ashley River—and the city of Charleston. I could even make out cars moving along what I learned later was Murray Boulevard on South Battery. To my left, and at the edge of the ploughed field, was a marshy low area of several acres through which a tiny stream wound off into a clump of trees.

I pulled on my clothes, woke my brother, and rushed downstairs. My mother was frying bacon on a two-burner oil stove and my father was kneeling in front of the fireplace in the dining room, his head enveloped with smoke. Starting a fire in a little basket grate was not as easy as he had anticipated—not as simple a task as starting a fire in a tight, well-drafted stove in Pennsylvania.

"You kids go out to the woodpile and see if you can find some old chips—not the kind that's just been cut." He was clearly exasperated. He picked up a piece of cardboard and began fanning the flicker of fire in the hearth. This made the fire flame up, but also sent up a cloud of dust to join the smoke in the room. "Get moving," he said.

We took a pail from the back porch and went down to where Ned was cutting wood. We looked around rather helplessly and then one of us said, "We're supposed to find some dry chips." Ned was pleasant but not sociable. Chopping wood was strenuous, and he needed all of his wind for his exertions.

"Look over behind dat chicken house," he said.

There we collected half a pail of weathered chips and returned to the house. With the help of some old newspapers and our dry chips, my father finally got a flame going up the chimney. I could see that he was already disenchanted with fireplaces. We stood around shivering and then he said, "You'd better get your sweaters."

We wandered onto the front porch, still vaguely seeking to be oriented. The house faced south on a grassy yard that was shaded by the two live oaks. A hundred feet beyond the trees a farm road ran east through the pasture until it disappeared in a grove of oaks. To our right, the road led to the plantation buildings a quarter of a mile away and to the shore of James Island Creek. It was here that we had left the Anderson car to greet Mrs. Lawton the afternoon before. Alison Lawton's house on whose porch we had stood and looked out over the marsh was not a pretentious or historic building. Its rooms were larger than those of the Cuthbert house, and hanging from the ceilings of the two downstairs rooms were large gas chandeliers that were fed from a small carbide generating plant nearby.

The buildings clustered along the high ground bordering the creek were fairly typical of those on James Island plantations of that day. A three-storied gin house at the water's edge, two wharves, several low rambling hay sheds, a watering trough, a windmill, a water tower, a collection of small buildings and feed-

ing lots. Adjacent to these buildings was a group of cabins that housed the Negro workers and their families. The Cuthbert house was pleasantly distanced from the plantation's working center; one could not walk the field road to the Bluff without involuntarily turning to the right to view the city skyline across the pasture. This was the matchless view of the Charleston peninsula that Mr. Lawton had mentioned in his letters.

Soon after we had swallowed our bacon and eggs and my father had started a fire in the kitchen cook stove, we were ready to accompany him to the Bluff—a name for the entire plantation but for us children the word meant the cluster of buildings on James Island Creek. "Can we go to the Bluff?" became a question that our parents would answer many times during our early years on James Island. There was always some kind of action at the Bluff, and that first morning was no exception. We came to the cow barns first where the dairy boys were cleaning up after the milk-

ing; my father led us past the empty stanchions where we met
Oscar and Eddie—tall, gangling boys who would be my friends
for the next ten years.

"Mornin' Mistuh Breezy." They grinned at us and we smiled
back. My father told them that we were his children, and mentioned our names.

"De bigges' boy look like you, suh," one of them said pleasantly.

"Yes, we've heard that before," my father replied.

We left Eddie and Oscar to walk over to the test barn. Here
Gillie Scott was caring for a group of cows that received special
rations and were milked three times a day.

"Mornin' Mistuh Breezy." Like Eddie and Oscar, he smiled
broadly when we were introduced. My father gave him some instructions on feeding and they went to examine a particular cow.
Having been on duty for three weeks before we arrived, my father
was now fully acquainted with the routine of the plantation. Gillie
had the most responsible job of all the workers. He had to carefully weigh the feed for each cow, record the pounds of milk produced, and bring the little herd to the barn at midnight for a
special milking. He had little else to do but care for twelve or
fifteen cows around the clock. He was able to read and write, skills
that were required of no others except the field foreman.

As we walked down toward the creek, my father said, "Gillie is
a good man. And you ought to hear him sing when he's doing the
midnight milking. I'm going to bring your mother down here
some night and have her listen to him. I'd like to know what the
people up North would say if they could hear him sing in one of
our big churches."

Gillie was a natural tenor—clear, limpid, effortless. I'm sure that
he never matched tones with a piano and had no idea what his
range might be, but I think now that he achieved easily the dream
of the great lyric tenors—a pianissimo high C.

We were standing on the gin house wharf looking at a small launch that was pulled up on the bank when Mr. Lawton walked down from his home and joined us.

"You know, Mr. Bresee, I think we ought to get the *Virginia* repaired and back in service," he said, looking down at the boat. "She mostly needs a good recaulking. We'll have to put a couple of men to work on her."

St. John Alison Lawton almost always began his remarks to my father with, "You know, Mr. Bresee . . ." I noticed that he was the first person we had met who pronounced our name correctly. Bresee is a French name and rhymes with foresee, but no Negro on James Island ever got it right. Our family name to them was the adjective for a pleasant, windy day! A few years ago, I discovered that a street on James Island bears our name. I drove the whole length of it, occasionally stopping to ask people at the roadside, "What street is this, please?" Invariably, the answer was "Breezy Street." We learned not to be annoyed at this because no one in the low country—black or white—pronounced the French Huguenot names of the area correctly. We would join such illustrious low-country names as Huger (Hew-Gee), Beaufain (Bew-Fane), Prioleau (Pray-Low), and Legare (Luh-Gree).

From the gin house we moved along the water's edge to the main plantation wharf—a planked structure that extended far enough into James Island Creek to permit boat landings.

"The tide is about half in now," Mr. Lawton told us while we looked at two rowboats just beginning to come awash. As we crept closer to the edge of the wharf to get a better look, we sent a flock of fiddler crabs scurrying for their holes in the mud. A wooden hoop with burlap sewed to it lay in a heap on the wharf— a decaying crab half-concealed in its folds.

"The children catch shrimp here in homemade dip nets," Mr. Lawton remarked. "The worse that bait smells, the more shrimp they will catch." I decided that as soon as I could manage to get away I would be down at the wharf shrimping. "The first thing you children must do," Mr. Lawton continued, "is to learn to swim. The best place for that is up at the little wharf by the gin house. Right now the air is a little chilly, but our spring comes early. But watch out for oyster shells; they'll slice you all up."

The shore end of the wharf was attached to the plantation commissary, or "the store," as everyone called it. The store was a rectangular, one-storied building with walls peeling whitewash, and built on brick piers for protection against the high tides. The windows were covered by solid wooden blinds painted red. The store porch and the wharf made a large two-level platform that I would soon see crowded with people on Friday nights.

"Mr. Knight should open up around ten o'clock," Mr. Lawton told us. "We sell mostly food and other necessities for our workers, although we draw customers from this end of the island." He turned to my father, "Mrs. Bresee will find that she can get many things that she needs right here in our own store."

In early afternoon, when we had grown tired of playing around the house, my brother and I asked permission to go back to the creek.

"Can we go down to the Bluff?"

"What do you want to do there?"

"Oh, just look around." Secretly, we wanted to go back to the water's edge. Our mother apparently suspected as much, for she said, "Will you promise not to play on the wharf?"

"We promise."

The sun was now shining hot on the fields as we followed the sandy field road toward the barns and dairy buildings. Several dozen cows, who took no notice of us, were drifting over a pasture that extended out to the marsh by the Ashley River; across the water we could see the housetops and steeples of Charleston. Just as we reached the cluster of buildings, our way was barred by a locked gate; beside the gate was a stile, the first one we had ever seen. A ladder over a fence! What a way to do things! I would discover later that the plantation had at least a dozen gates, many with padlocks and a few with stiles. Climbing back and forth over the fence detained us for a few minutes, but we pressed on to the creek. We reached the water's edge between the gin house and the wharf. The tide was far out and we stood still for a few moments trying to see everything at once. To have this shoreline for a playground was almost unbelievable. This living, warm thing before us and a stream of moving water! The sloping plane of mud, popping in the hot sun; the black surface skimming with fiddler crabs that vanished like raindrops when we approached. Some of the fiddler crabs had big claws slung along their front sides—whichever their front was; they could dart backward or forward with equal speed. Below the gin house at our right, a big white bird with long legs and a long beak stood in the shallow water staring at us severely.

There had been nothing like this up North. The only water I had been near was a cold lake where our family gathered for a Fourth-of-July picnic. There had been a big dinner at tables on a grassy knoll under the trees, then a cautious walk on the pebbled shore—always firmly attached to someone's hand. We were allowed to remove our shoes and socks and walk for a few minutes in the cold water, while the big boys skipped stones on the lake. But never before so much life and warmth as this!

We were not alone, for down at the wharf two Negro boys were fishing—seated at the very end with their legs dangling. They probably knew how to swim, we thought, but actually they were sitting almost above the mud, so low was the water. Venturing out

to talk with them would hardly be breaking our promise, because you couldn't fall off and drown in the mud. Without any real discussion of the matter, however, we decided to stay on shore.

We moved toward the gin house and the big white bird. He turned slowly as if he were fed up with us, unfolded bigger wings than we had ever seen before, and flapped out of sight around the bend in the creek. The shoreline was different here; firm damp ground covered with short marsh grass was under our feet now. The high water did not apparently get in this far—or not so often. We watched a little band of fiddler crabs feeding beside their holes.

"These don't have big claws," my brother said, "let's catch one."

We took off our shoes and socks and stepped onto the damp ground. After lunging back and forth for a few minutes, we surprised a little crab too far from his hole. We took turns holding his square little body, his tiny mandibles fighting bravely against our fingertips.

"Is it a father or a mother crab?" my brother asked.

"I don't know," I said. "Let's look." We turned him over carefully, checking all sides, but could find no clues.

"I don't know how to tell," I said. "Maybe they're the same." We put him on the ground and he shot backward into the grass.

We inched our way closer to the creek. The black ooze came up between our toes, and it was here that I had my first brush with buried oyster shells—not a cut, but a good scratch.

I thought as I stood in the mud that I had never seen so much sky at one time. Instead of starting at the top of the nearest hill, it began far away across the marsh at a pencil line of trees and stretched out right and left with nothing for my eyes to rest on.

Water and sky and mud banks and birds held us all afternoon— so long that someone at home got worried. My mother came down to the Bluff to see for herself. On the way down she picked up my father and they decided to go to the creek. They did not find us at once because we were half-concealed behind the gin house. There was a sigh of relief in my mother's voice.

"Well, there you are at last. Are you all right?"

"Sure we're all right. We didn't go out on the wharf."

My father seemed less worried and only asked if we thought we'd like it here.

"Look at your feet! Dear, I do worry about this creek."

"There's only one solution," my father said as we started for home. "We'll teach these boys to swim."

The overriding question of that first day for my sister and me was "Where do we go to school?" Mr. Lawton had said that there was a good two-room school a couple of miles from the border of his plantation, which might make it nearly three miles from home. How would we get there? The answer, reduced to its simplest terms was, "It's up to you—there are no buses." Some children drove a buggy to school—the Bresees would eventually—some got a ride with a neighbor, one or two rode horseback. I was soon to notice that white people rarely walked along public roads; the Negroes had to walk because, for the most part, they had no other means of transportation, but I soon gained the impression that it would be unseemly for planters' children to participate so openly in this ancient social leveler—traveling afoot at the roadside.

My parents therefore needed to find someone to take us to James Island Grammar School; in a few months we would acquire a Dodge touring car, but for the next few weeks? Perhaps, Mr. Lawton suggested, we could get Tate Seabrook, an eighteen-year-old youth who had a temporary job at the Bluff, to take us in his little runabout car. He owned a topless little coupé with a rumble seat. Some arrangement must have been consummated, because on the next Monday morning the little coupé stopped in front of our house and a smiling young man said, "Hop in!"

My chief impression of those trips to school was that Tate had made a bet with someone that he could make the round trip in ten minutes. When he had pulled away from the buildings, he would say, "Now I'm going to open 'er up," and then he would open the cutout valve, which allowed the engine exhaust to bypass the muffler. The explosions in the cylinders hit our ears like a thunderclap, and with its new burst of power the little car would roar down the sandy road, lurching so wildly that at times we were nearly thrown out of the rumble seat. We were not frightened because Tate would turn his good-looking face around to us and say with a grin, "How you-all coming back there? Just stay with me a few minutes longer." Then he would return to his driving just in time to bring his wheels back into the sand rut with a jerk. I think he was paid twenty-five cents a day.

Although Tate Seabrook became a sort of hero to us, we made the mistake of talking at the supper table about the hair-raising rides, sparing no details. My parents seem to have taken immediate action, for we were soon told that thereafter a planter at Clark's Point who had two boys of school age would drive us to James Island Grammar School.

During the first few weeks at James Island school we were Yankees, who caused great amusement by our pronunciation of words like "wat-ter" and "pa-perr." There were a few skirmishes in the early weeks that might begin with: *Clyde's a Yankee, Clyde's a Yankee—I'd rather be a Yankee than a Rebel—Oh yeah?—We beat you up once—You couldn't do it again*—followed by a few tentative punches. Everyone was glad to end the fracas quickly, because none of us came from families where fighting was tolerated.

Neither could we call the school principal "Cousin Martha," as half of the other children did. A dozen plantations comprised the larger part of James Island—Stono, Whitehouse, Centerville, Seaside, Secessionville, Oyster Point, to name a few—and nearly all of them sent children to James Island Grammar School. Of this group of children, the ones that I knew best were related.

This phalanx of James Island planters could have presented a formidable obstacle to our social progress in the community, but in fact it did not. Overtures of friendship came from all sides. These school families were also the church families; the parents of my friends were pillars in the Presbyterian or Episcopal churches, which the Bresees began to attend on alternate Sundays of the month, as was the James Island custom. The same group belonged to the newly formed PTA, of which my mother soon became president, and her friends belonged to the Ladies Auxiliary of the

Southern Presbyterian Church. The James Island Agricultural Society, the Parent Teachers Association, and the little churches were
one. For us youngsters, the overlap of the James Island Grammar
School, the Sunday school, and the Christian Endeavor Society
was almost complete.

Experts in social psychology could not have devised a setting
that could more speedily have transformed a Yankee boy into a
Southerner—or at least the James Island version of one. I fell in
love with grits and red rice at first taste, although I drew the line
at clabber laced with cinnamon and sugar.

## 3

# *Tip Your Hat to Ladies*

In James Island School nearly every boy wore a cap. We didn't wear them to keep warm, surely; it was just another of those odd clothing customs that exist the world over. We even wore them to recess, because I can see us now filing by a row of nails in the corridor, each boy hooking his hat over one as we walked into the classroom. We may have worn caps back in Pennsylvania, but I know one thing for certain, we didn't tip them to ladies. If my parents had called me aside and told me that here in the South I must tip my hat, I am not sure how successful their instruction would have been. They did not need to, because I watched the boys at school. The first time, of course, mine was the only hand that remained motionless when a lady approached a group of us at play. But not the second time. Hat tipping and handshaking were what impressed me most about all the men and boys I knew when I first arrived on James Island.

The James Island planters were the handshakingest group of men I had ever seen. This custom was most conspicuous in the churchyard, where tipping their hats—some men actually removed them for a moment—and shaking hands kept the men busy for the first few minutes as they gathered under the trees before service. A handshake can mean many things—greeting, pledge, reconciliation, parting. For us boys on the playground it meant mainly pledge and reconciliation—"O.K., shake on it"—or after a squabble someone would say, "Why don't you shake hands and make up?" We hadn't watched these men for nothing.

I soon learned that a girl was more special on James Island than up North. Entering a room of mixed company, she rated the same treatment as a lady—you rose and made a little gesture of offering her your chair. Even I had been taught that if there was no place for a newcomer to sit, you offered your seat—unless it was your sister, in which case she could fend for herself—but on James Island something was added. There might be three vacant chairs available, but a boy stood up anyhow for the perfectly obvious reason—she was a girl.

And on James Island school ground a boy never swore in the presence of girls. I can't remember that I was ever admonished for not being properly restrained in their presence, but we had a playmate from Folly Island area, more given to obscenities or swearing than the others, who would often merit a "Cut it out—there's girls present." When they were out of range, the ban was lifted.

Sometime in those first months on James Island I lost my way of referring to adults by their first names. Back in Pennsylvania, even as a small child I could have called people on the next farm Mike and Helen as my parents did. Not on James Island. Had I not heard of the words "Mr." and "Mrs."? Years were to elapse before even my mother's friends were to replace Mrs. Bresee with Ruth. For my friends, the omnipresent word "Cousin" solved the problem of a proper title, but for me it was Mr. and Mrs. to the end. The reluctance to use familiar first names until after long acquaintance has persisted in me to this day. I wince inwardly when after a few weeks' acquaintance I hear people call the new pastor "Bill." I had been brought up to wait a little longer.

My parents, too, had much to learn in working with and directing the black people on the plantation. My father was not only manager but he was also herdsman; it was his expertise in dairy husbandry that St. John Alison Lawton had sought when he hired him. He must know pedigrees and general herd improvement policies, and he must also know cows—almost individually. A Negro youth milking the cows, unless continually supervised, would never detect and report an udder problem. A dairy cow at the height of her milk production cycle needs constant observation by a knowledgeable person. This kind of attention cannot be given from horseback, or in a discussion with the foreman. The same may be said of calving and feeding.

St. John Alison Lawton conceived of his manager as indeed a manager, and sometimes showed annoyance at my father's tendency to step in and perform a task himself rather than to instruct a Negro worker who might or might not do the job satisfactorily. If Mr. Bresee was to pass as manager—and planter—there were a few customs he must observe.

Once a cistern or holding tank was being prepared next to the pasteurizing building. An excavation ten or twelve feet deep and large enough to hold several men at work was about to accommodate a wooden form that was being lowered. The men at the bottom of the pit were having trouble, and my father jumped down to help. No sooner had he done this than Mr. Lawton accompanied by his banker and a friend from the city drove up. Mr. Lawton was much displeased. Later he was supposed to have said, "Now Mr. Bresee, I was quite embarrassed the other day. I brought my friends over to meet my new manager and I found him in a muddy hole. You should direct some of the hands to do that kind of work for you."

Then there was the matter of a horse. On large plantations such as ours there was really no way of keeping an eye on the crops and the pastures without some means of transportation. Two-wheeled mule carts were abundant on the Bluff; they were the equivalent of the little trucks and jeeps of today. But the manager could hardly supervise the plantation from a mule cart, and no one expected him to. The only solution was a horse; soon word went out to all the dealers in the area that a saddle horse was needed at the Bluff. My father spent several weeks visiting sales lots and finally came home with a stalwart, deep-chested riding horse with a silky, chestnut coat. His name was Prince. His previous owner had taught him the art of single-footing, and we had great fun watching my father put him through his paces in the pasture. Ned, of course, cared for him and would bring him saddled to our house on the days when my father rode out to inspect the plantation. Mounted upon this large, handsome saddle horse, my father came noticeably closer to St. John Alison Lawton's concept of a manager.

My mother soon learned that all her friends had cooks and washerwomen. Up North my mother had employed a "hired girl" to help her for a few months when babies came, but the notion of a full-time cook was new and exciting. When my father asked the field foreman which families might provide us such a worker, he was advised to talk to Sam Davis; Sam had an intelligent wife who managed her children well, and she had two teenage daughters who would like a job. We would therefore try the oldest daughter, Azalee, for a week. Azalee came on a Monday morning in December for a week that lasted for the rest of our stay on James Island—and she stayed on in our hearts forever. Quick to learn, eager to succeed and blessed with a quiet sense of humor and a soft winning giggle, Azalee became one of us.

As for the washing, my mother could not bring herself to send it out to one of the little cabins where a woman would wash it with water heated over an open fire, iron it with a charcoal-heated flatiron, and return it a week later. Instead, she hired Lucy to come every Monday and do the washing on our own back porch. Azalee could do the ironing.

An older woman, Lucy, arrived smoking a pipe, which she tucked in the depths of her many skirts as she reached our house. She spent the better part of a day scrubbing on the washboard and talking to herself in a barely audible jumble. When we children talked to her, she replied in what at the time was an unintelligible Gullah dialect. I think we annoyed her, and she never became a part of our family. She would have much preferred to take the clothes home to wash in her own leisurely style, freed of my mother's steady supervision.

An episode soon convinced us why our clothes had to be washed on our own back porch. One morning I heard my mother fairly scream—for she rarely raised her voice—"Lucy! What are you doing? Dump those clothes out right now!" Now Lucy often had a cold on her chest and did a lot of coughing—probably from smoking. Watching from the kitchen window, my mother had seen Lucy develop a fit of coughing, raise a mouthful of phlegm, and spit it into the tub of clothes. My mother rushed out the door, started to tip over the tub on the back porch, but restrained herself. "Get fresh water and wash all those clothes over! Don't you ever do such a filthy thing again!" Poor, troubled Lucy. I'm not sure that she ever knew what the fuss was about.

We were moving steadily closer to the James Island norm. My mother was relieved of all burdensome housework; she could even come to the kitchen in the morning and find the fire started, and breakfast well under way; her afternoons were now free for driving around the island in the new Dodge. Duties were steadily lifted from the children. There was little or no housework for my sister except to care for her room. Ned chopped the wood, but my brother and I had to keep the kitchen wood box full. We were also required to throw out a few handfuls of corn to our little flock of mongrel chickens twice a day—such onerous, heavy work that we quarreled about it. Work on a family farm had been my parents' model for generations, yet here there was simply no work for us children to do. It must have troubled them.

As for my brother and myself, we perceived nothing amiss with our way of life. Off with our shoes in April and barefoot until Thanksgiving—except when we went to church. Our feet became so calloused that they were impervious to everything but oyster shells.

School was out by two and our dinner was over by three. The plantation was ours until supper time. We had the choice of the pleasures of the wharf—fishing, shrimping, crabbing, the tidal inlet behind the house, the two shallow ponds in the pasture, the mud banks for "bogging." Best of all, there was hunting with the air rifle. My father tried to teach us to shoot at pictures in a Sears Roebuck catalogue, tame pleasures that soon gave away to shooting at moving targets—the multitudes of little birds that darted in the thickets of cassena bushes. Why shoot at a pair of shoes in the catalogue when you could creep into a hedgerow and take aim at a song sparrow jumping about in the twigs over your head? We did, however, conduct our sport with a little honor—we never shot at cardinals or mockingbirds. They were too big to be brought down by a BB gun and it wouldn't be right to leave one maimed.

Hunting was always good in the thickets down at the tide. One Saturday morning I took careful aim at a grayish brown bird perched on a strand of rusty fence. It fell to the ground without flap or flutter; it just dropped dead, shot by my own hand. My brother and I raced to the spot, picked it up, found where the lethal bullet had struck, and passed the limp carcass back and forth with a new sense of exultation and power—especially of power.

We went after loggerhead shrikes with an almost religious fervor, although they are difficult to kill with an air rifle. These evil birds with their crooked beak, large eyes, and harsh coloring would rob the nests of other birds and impale the little birdlings on the spikes of a barbed wire fence. We could find the shrunken, dried-up little skulls anytime we looked for them, and the sight always filled us with righteous outrage. But shrikes rarely sat over our heads in a thicket, and they were hard to bring down perched far away on a fence. The little greenish birds, ruby-crowned kinglets and warblers, were our favorite targets. And you could always take a shot at a black cat. Like shrikes, they deserved a sudden death by any means, for there was hardly a person on the Bluff who did not believe that a black cat crossing your path caused bad luck. Away with them—anytime you saw one—although a BB gun would only make a black cat run faster!

I hunted birds with a fierce intensity then—an intensity that in only a few years would leave without a trace, never to return. Did I grow up? I have decided since that I did. I have concluded sadly that the adults whom I hear telling with almost visceral pleasure of how a little animal was brought to earth by their own hand are still locked in that primitive passion of childhood.

Our activities ranged over so broad an area and were so varied that even parents as protective as ours could not possibly monitor all our activities. They did not know about cottonmouth moccasins, so how could they warn or worry about us as we played around brackish water, or slept on the ground in nests of Spanish moss? If we climbed too high in the soft limbs of chinaberry trees, there was only our good sense to tell us to back away when the branch began to crack. Seeing us up to our knees in banks of black muck when the tide was out would probably have disturbed them.

But they had not seen the mud bank. They might learn of our afternoon "bogging" only if one of our feet had hit an oyster shell buried in the muck; wash the cut in the bath tub, limp a few days, and it was better. Band-Aids had not been invented then. We were not sneakily disobeying rules—we were exploring farther and farther afield everyday, and anything that looked like fun and seemed only a little dangerous was worth a try.

We first met Jamsie late one afternoon when we were crabbing down at the gin house. The creek was now a quiet lake that stretched for nearly a mile in front of us, with only the tips of the marsh grass showing above the surface. Jamsie, dressed in an oversized shirt and tattered knee pants, stood barefoot, ankle-deep in water that was spreading thinly into the low grass around us. He had a pail, a garden rake, and a length of cord with bait tied to the end, as did my brother and I. And then in the manner of small boys and old men alike, we began a conversation with talk of our catch—Jamsie had more crabs than we had.

"How many you got?"

"'Bout seven, I tink."

"Gee—they're big."

"Dey not so big."

"What's your name?"

"Jamsie."

"Jamsie who?"

"Jamsie Walker. Who y'all is?"

"I'm Clyde and he's Kenneth. He's my brother."

"Bet y'all is de new folks dat jus' come from up North." He gave us a wondering look and a half smile.

"Yeah. We never caught crabs before."

"Y'all ain't got no crabs up North?"

"No. We don't have any salt water or tides or anything like this," I said.

Jamsie had long arms and legs that made him seem bigger than he actually was. He grinned at us as if he liked us, and we moved closer to watch him work. He would toss his bait into the shallow water that extended about ten feet from the shore, and in a moment two claws would flash out of the water and hang on. Then he would gently tug the bait and crab toward shore—until within range of his rake. We followed the same procedure, but few crabs took hold of our bait, a piece of salt pork from our kitchen.

"You need better bait," Jamsie said, "somethin' that stinks real bad." He had on the end of his line a dead fish that fully met his specifications. "Dey like anything dat's rotten. If you can get some smoked herring, dat's awful good, too." Then he added, "But you got to buy dat." I soon learned that Jamsie didn't buy many things.

"Hold my line," he said to my brother. "I get you some bettah bait."

He handed his string to Kenneth, and I followed Jamsie down to the wharf. He grabbed the line of a rowboat and pulled it in close, jumped in the boat, splashed around in the leak-water, and in a moment clambered up on the wharf with a dead fish in his hand. Back by the gin house I helped him tie it tightly against my piece of salt pork. "Dat butts-meat not so good, but we leave it dere," he said. We wrapped the crumbling, half-decayed fish with string until it was secure.

I tried to wash my hands in the creek water. Jamsie laughed. "Maybe you don' like dat smell, but de crabs sho' do."

He was right. The big claws began breaking the water at the end of our string, and we were crabbing in earnest.

Crabbing at high tide after school was, we were to learn, a severely limited activity. "Let's crab again tomorrow," we said to him—"right after school." We did not know that the tides would be an hour later tomorrow; an hour later would put us close to supper time. Three days at the most for crabbing after school were all we could expect, given the parameters.

Jamsie met us at the tidal inlet behind our house a few days later. My brother and I were wading in the shallow stream when we saw him standing up by the barns. We yelled across the pasture for him to join us. There were not many crabs in the water at dead low tide, and the ones we found were small. We waded around for a while in the shallow stream that had now been reduced to a trickle. We impounded some small shrimp in a little boy-made pool, then turned to chasing fiddlers. Suddenly, Jamsie said, "Let's hunt fo' cuddahs. We haf to get yo' rake fo' dat."

"What are cuddahs?" we asked.

"Dey 'bout dis big around." He made a circle about a foot in diameter. "Dey have a hard shell. I show you. Les get de rake firs'."

In a few minutes he was taking us across the big pasture in front of our house to a little well-like structure in the ground that was about six feet deep and about three feet square with boarded sides. This little "well" served as a gathering point or junction for the network of drainage tiles that underlay the plantation fields. This was what Mr. Lawton had meant in his letter by the statement, "My place has all underground drainage."

We dropped on our knees at the edge of the "well" and looked in. Turtles! A half dozen of them with shells as large as dinner plates were resting on the bottom. Clear water about a foot deep was moving gently across yellow sand. The cuddah, I would learn later, was a species of freshwater edible terrapin, but Jamsie already knew this. Using our rake, we pulled one up and dumped it on the grass. Jamsie turned it over and held it while we studied its yellow underside. Jamsie had plans to take it home for his mother to cook, but we had nothing in which to carry it.

"Let's get Mom's washtub," my brother volunteered.

We watched the cuddah lumber back to the well and tumble in with a splash, and then headed to our house for the tub. No need to ask permission, we reasoned. My mother was sensible about such things—we wouldn't harm the tub and we'd bring it back soon. An hour later Jamsie and I were walking across the pasture bearing the tub between us while my brother followed behind with a stick to push the turtles back if they tried to climb out. We created a big stir at the back porch, but Jamsie did not linger. We gave him an old feed bag into which he put three turtles, and started across the pasture for home. After my family had admired the remaining three, we released them down at the inlet.

Jamsie knew what we had not yet learned—that he should not play at our house. At the wharf, with the boats, down at the tidal inlet, in the fields, anywhere but our house was all right. We liked to be with him and, quite unaware that we were doing so, quickly adapted to the restrictions. Any spot was more interesting than our dooryard—and doubly so, if Jamsie could play with us.

# 4

# *Destroyed by the Enemy*

If you stand on Charleston's famous Battery and look south across the Ashley River, you see the shoreline of James Island stretching from Fort Johnson at the harbor entrance westward to the twin bridges that cross the Ashley. Squarely in the center of this range, occupying over a half mile of waterfront, was the Lawton plantation. From my upstairs bedroom window in the Cuthbert house, I could see the harbor nearly to Fort Sumter, and the city of Charleston lying low on the peninsula. I was separated from it by a cultivated field, a stretch of marsh, and the Ashley River. Only partially aware as a child of the dramas that had been played out on these lands and waters, I nevertheless sensed the enchantment of this spot. I was to spend many hours at this window over the ten years of my stay on James Island. No books or toys in that bedroom could match the attractions of the north window. In the morning I watched and heard the city come alive, noted what ships had arrived and checked the state of the tide in the inlet below the house. If fog had settled in during the night, I would hear the nervous toots of the harbor traffic, or the lordly, drawn-out call of a big steamer at the jetties demanding entrance to the port. Before going to bed at night, I would lean on the broad sill of the dormer window for a last look. There I would absorb the night sounds in the live oaks behind me, the glimmering lights on

the battery, the muffled hum of the city, and the intermittent tin-
kling of a buoy at the mouth of James Island Creek.

We had moved into one of the oldest houses on James Island;
indeed, into one of the oldest houses in the Carolina low country.
Erected on a gentle knoll in the surrounding fields, it faced south
and the two historic live oaks. Thomas Heyward, father of the
signer of the Declaration of Independence, built the house in 1747
for his daughter, who married a Cuthbert; the house was subse-
quently known by that name. It was not the colonnaded mansion
one sees in picture books of "the old South"—there weren't many
such dwellings in 1747—but a Dutch Colonial frame house. Massive, identical, brick chimneys stood at each end of the house;
between them were gambrel roofs with four dormer windows on
each side. The house was bilaterally symmetrical whichever way
you sliced it. I have often wondered how it survived the hurricanes of two centuries and the famous earthquake of 1886. I suspect those two massive chimneys—made of bricks twice the size
of modern bricks—may have had much to do with keeping the
house upright.

The ground floor of the Cuthbert house consisted of two large
rooms—one on each side of an entrance hall, which contained a
small curving staircase; upstairs, another pair of rooms nearly
matched those on the first floor, with space taken out for a hall
and a smaller room. There was a fireplace in each of the four large
rooms. A kitchen was attached to the rear, and there was an un-
impressive porch across the front.

Its location on a slight rise of ground behind the two handsome
oaks in the front yard partially compensated for what, by modern
standards, was poor design. In another sense, the builders knew
what they were doing. It was similar to many houses in Charleston
that were known as "single houses"—houses that were one room
thick. Such a design was the "air conditioning" of the time—

breezes could flow freely through the rooms and especially across the beds at night. When we came to live on James Island, the Cuthbert house had been standing on its little knoll for one hundred and seventy-five years. Its basic structure had not changed to the present day. There had been a new roof, the kitchen annex and front porch had no doubt been repaired, but the house itself had remained steady between the massive chimneys.

My bedroom, with its north window, had been in existence for thirty years when the British ships sailed into Charleston Harbor on a June day in 1776. Men had climbed St. Michael's steeple hourly and looked through its circular windows to see whether the ships offshore had begun to move. When the British fleet of eleven ships sailed into the harbor, who had stood watching at my window? Through the early summer of 1776 a fleet of thirty vessels had been anchored offshore while its officers tried to decide when and if they should attack. There was even hope in England that the presence of His Majesty's forces might spur many Royalists in the southern colonies to side with the King, or at least refuse to take up arms against the mother country. It was a vain hope, for the colonists perceived this show of force as only another threat to their liberties.

While the fleet waited offshore, General Moultrie on a little point of land overlooking the harbor entrance was frantically assembling palmetto logs into a fort that would later bear his name. On the morning of June 28 the British launched their attack. The ships, under the command of Sir Peter Parker sailed up the channel and opened fire on the new fort. The understaffed garrison, short on powder, decided to concentrate their fire on the command ships. The green soldiers fired with uncommon accuracy, and in return the ships pounded the little fort mercilessly. Crowds gathered on the Charleston battery—then only earthworks—to try to discern through the smoke of the battle whether General

Moultrie's flag was flying over the fort. This was the battle when, according to my history books, the cannonballs bounced off the spongy palmetto logs, and Sgt. Jasper restored the fallen flag to the top of the merlon. The accurate fire of the land-based cannons decimated the British fleet, and the ships withdrew around midnight during an intense thunderstorm. A local historian wrote: "That an English admiral, with a well-appointed fleet of two hundred and seventy guns, should be beaten off by a miserable little half-built fort on an uninhabited sand bank, was incomprehensible." But as General Moultrie modestly said, "They did not know the resisting quality of our palmetto wood." He might also have added that "resisting quality" on that day was not confined to palmetto wood.

Four years later Charleston would be attacked again, and this time the city would fall to the enemy. General Clinton, profiting by the mistakes of the first attack, landed an army on our neighboring Johns Island and proceeded to encircle the city from the south and west. At sea, a large fleet had been assembled which now, with tides and winds favorable, sailed swiftly up the channel until the ships came within range of the city itself—not pausing to respond to fire from Fort Moultrie. The plight of the colonists, crowded into the end of the Charleston peninsula, was hopeless. The final night of battle was called in my history books a night of horror. Two hundred pieces of heavy artillery were fired at the same time; mortars from British forts on James Island—in particular one known as "watermelon battery" located not far from the Cuthbert house—did great damage to the lower end of the city. An observer wrote: "It was a glorious sight to see the shells like meteors crossing each other, and bursting in the air; it appeared as if the stars were falling to the earth. The firing was incessant all night long. The British threw red hot cannon balls and contrivances called 'carcasses' from their mortars. A carcass was an iron frame which carried combustibles and burst into blaze as it fell. So many houses were of wood that the effect was terrible."

From my upstairs window I, too, watched rockets—but no cannonballs—rise and explode over the city. Every New Year's Eve, when the people of Charleston discharged their fireworks, my family gathered on the second floor of our house to watch the spectacle. Hundreds of rockets and Roman candles soared above the skyline and burst. It was not hard for me to imagine another night when a frightened family might have watched the siege of Charleston from this very window.

The Cuthbert house would see three generations pass before another war came to the Sea Islands. Its history in this period—and that of the surrounding acres—is not clear. In 1813 Winborn Lawton acquired the lands that came to be known as Lawton's Bluff, making a plantation bordered on one side by James Island Creek and on the adjacent side by the Ashley River. Neighboring lands were added during these intervening years, and the elegant Bennett house was built by the edge of the harbor.

The Civil War came to the Sea Islands within a year after the outbreak of hostilities. The secession movement had begun in South Carolina, and the defiant Charlestonians in particular must be made to suffer. The Union forces sought control of the waterways around the city. Federal gunboats patrolled the low country rivers, and found easy opportunity for shelling and the landing of troops as they plied the meandering streams. The defenders erected a string of breastworks and gun emplacements called batteries along the water courses, the remains of which were fascinating playgrounds for us as children. These fortifications, however, could not keep out the invader, and the James Island planters fled inland. Wallace Lawton, who was then planting on the lands I was

to know, gathered his slaves and moved to Lawtonville, near Beaufort, South Carolina.

It was here that Wallace, father of St. John Alison, met his future wife, Cecilia—a peppery lady of whom I heard my father speak often. She became years later the owner of the Battery Dairy, marketing agent for the milk produced on the Bluff. She died in 1923 in Charleston, at the age of seventy-six. If the burned plantation homes and the earthworks that lurked in the James Island hedgerows had not been enough to preserve the memory of those troubled days, Cecilia Lawton's diary, kept during the years from 1860 to 1870, would have done so.*

She enters our story with the first mention of her future husband, Wallace, a man eleven years her senior: "He had recently bought a large plantation near Lawtonville (six miles off) and moved his slaves there, having been ordered to move them from James Island by the Confederate General in charge."

She writes in much detail of Wallace's "constant attention" to her: "He always called upon me accompanied by his body servant, Cain, dressed in a full suit of black broadcloth, for few affected liveries in those days." She notes that he had left his army outfit, known as the Rutledge Mounted Riflemen, because he was recovering from a prolonged attack of "typhoid-malaria fever." The remaining several years of hostilities were not sufficient time for recovery, it appears, because he never returned to military life.

Wallace's courtship of the sixteen-year-old Cecilia was apparently swift and vigorous, for she states that their engagement to marry came "about six weeks after our first meeting." Later, when she is telling of her family's opposition to the union, she notes— apparently to convince the reader that desperation did not drive

---

*This diary, which I only heard about as a child, I have had the good fortune to read in later years. It is now owned by Mrs. Lavinia Royall Campbell of Charleston, who has kindly permitted me to quote from it.

her into Wallace's arms—that by the age of sixteen she had received three offers of marriage. Although not part of our story, there are a dozen entries in the journal that tell of the disillusionment and grief that Wallace caused her.

During the courtship, Wallace made a mistake that nearly cost him his fiancée. While driving with Cecilia one evening, he allowed the carriage to jolt badly in a mud puddle. "Wallace passed his arm around my waist saying jokingly that he was afraid I would fall out." She writes that she was furious at him "because of this impertinence" and that she refused to see him for several days.

A week later she had sufficiently recovered from her "fury" to allow him to call upon her again, for she reports that they were sitting on the piazza of a country residence "on a perfect night— the moon making it bright as day." With the moon as his ally, Wallace quickly regained lost ground, and they continued their plans for marriage.

At sixteen, the product of a private girls' school and of a household attended by slaves, Cecilia found her new duties as plantation mistress quite overwhelming. Shortly after her marriage, she was to preside over a dinner party for Wallace's family and friends. When dinner was announced, she was to take her place at the head of the table opposite her husband. The sudden picture of herself as hostess and mistress of the plantation "and the fearful responsibilities of the life I had entered upon seemed to loom up before me suddenly, and I became hysterical." How the dinner party went from this point on, she does not state.

She was particularly disturbed by the thought that the "spinning and weaving of clothing for the slaves" was her responsibility; most frightening of all was the prospect of seeing that the slaves were cared for in sickness and in childbirth. She recoiled at punishing them, she writes, because "I was a child and a tender-hearted one."

She recounts in shocking detail the destruction of both her father's home and Wallace's plantation by Sherman's army, a loss that ultimately would force them to return to the old Lawton plantation home on James Island. Except for some horses, cattle, and the slaves, they were now destitute and lived in constant fear that the slaves would become lawless and destroy their animals.

A short time after Lee's surrender, they managed to move their few possessions to a safer area. The only house they could find for shelter was an unused Negro cabin, and here they set up housekeeping, using "a few sticks of furniture which the negroes had snatched from our burning house."

Then came the announcement of emancipation to the little farm. Wallace gathered his slaves about him and, standing on a cart, told them that the war was over and that they were now as free as he was. If they would agree to work for him for one year, they could have one-third share of the crops. According to Cecilia, "They received the speech in sullen silence, for they were eager to return to their former home on James Island. But they soon saw the reasonableness of his offer, since they were penniless, and all signed the contract. They might thus return to their home on the Sea Island in the fall with a little money in their pockets."

We must not suppose that the transition from slavery to freedom was as smooth as this episode suggests. Cecilia writes in 1865: "I regret to say that Wallace frequently forgot himself and administered corporal punishment to them [the ex-slaves]. It was both wrong and dangerous, but the old spirit of command remained."

For months the Lawtons were harassed by bands of blacks and Union soldiers who sought continually to lure the ex-slaves away from their work with promises that "Uncle Sam got 'nuf meat, sugar and coffee for you all. You fool to work any more. Come wid us." After one of these pleas, Wallace's entire force of workers dropped their plows and hoe handles and fled. In less than thirty minutes the plantation was deserted. After a few days, however, a number did return and the first crop was harvested.

Cecilia writes of another harrowing episode while they were living in the slave cabin:

On a bright sunny day, I was twisting some homespun thread on a spinning wheel and Wallace was reading, when I saw a squad of U.S. negro troops with bayonets presented, charging at double quick right upon Wallace. With wonderful control he showed no terror and sternly demanded their business. One of them stepped forward and said, "We come to tell you the slaves are free. You got no right to work 'em any more."

Wallace replied that they are free and they are working under contract.

A black soldier stepped up and asked him if he had taken the pledge of allegiance to the United States; finding out that he had not, the soldier took him to their white captain who released him upon a verbal promise to take the oath at his earliest convenience.

The following year Wallace and many of his former slaves moved back to James Island, and it is here that the house in which the Bresees lived enters the story. "It was a lovely spring day in the middle of March," she writes, "when Wallace took me over to James Island to live." They crossed the Ashley River in a rowboat, Cecilia holding her baby to her breast and weeping. This child was Alison, the man who hired my father.

She wept, perhaps, because she knew that they were returning to another scene of destruction and would have to rebuild their lives once again. Wallace's large plantation house at Bennetts (the easternmost section of the plantation) had been destroyed along with all outbuildings and trees. Then comes a detail that was not well known—at least, not well circulated in my day: "Our own soldiers—those belonging to the 'country cracker' class, who hated all wealthy planters—had wrought this destruction. Some of the places on James Island were destroyed by the Yankees also, so that, from friends and enemies, that doomed island suffered the worst."

The only buildings of any size left standing on Wallace's three James Island places (the Bluff, Cuthbert, and Bennetts—now fused into one) were a little two-room cottage on James Island Creek and the Cuthbert house. "The latter was badly out of repair and shunned by everyone because 500 negroes had died there of smallpox." A few years later Wallace and Cecilia would move into this house, although on their arrival they took lodging in the little two-room cottage. "Wallace, with his usual thrift, soon started a small store at the Bluff and sent for Robbie Oswald to clerk for him. He also made a little money every day by taking passengers to and from the city in a *long* boat called the 'Stark Naked,' so named because of its trim appearance. He had recovered the boat from some negroes who had stolen it from his James Island place during his 'refugeeing' absence."

Wallace emerges in these journals as a shrewd, driving man—from his unrelenting courtship days to the rehabilitation of his ruined plantation. At Lawtonville he had invested money in tobacco, which he sold to the destitute people at a great profit. When he found that the ex-slaves would not work for a former owner on James Island, he rented his fields "to a German for 1,000 dollars." He showed his shrewdness, bordering on the unscrupulous, in another way. In "buying back" his lands from the Negroes during the Reconstruction days he ended up with more than he had originally. Perhaps only such people could hold their own in those times. Wallace's hotheadedness and short temper were vividly described to me by my James Island friends who had known him. He was a compulsive gambler and usually carried sidearms. His ability to "close a deal" in his favor was legendary. Whatever shortcomings he may have had seem not to have interfered with his ability to acquire money and property. Doubtless he carried always the memory of his beautiful house at Bennetts that was destroyed during the occupation of James Island.

On Sunday afternoons in early spring a favorite walk for my family was out to Bennetts along the harbor front in search of spring flowers. We would make our way through a grove of live oaks, over a causeway through the marsh, across a wide pasture, coming finally to the water's edge. Among the bricks that marked the ruin of the old house, we gathered the first snowdrops and daffodils. The Bennett house, we had been told many times, was one of the truly fine houses of the Sea Islands. Mrs. Alison Lawton told us sadly one afternoon, as she visited the site with us, that "it was destroyed by the enemy," a delicately worded statement for the ears of these newcomers from the North. If she knew the facts from her mother-in-law's diary, as I assume she did, she nevertheless left the impression that the enemy was the Union army.

One passage in Cecilia's diary mentions a man whom I knew personally—Peter Brown, a former slave: "Black men roamed the island terrifying the few planters and in particular seeking vengeance on those who they thought had mistreated slaves. I recalled the blood-curdling stories . . . of these brutal-looking black men; and the fact that Wallace had that day beat Peter Brown, one of his former slaves."

During my stay on James Island I would come to know Peter Brown well. He was "Uncle Peter" to everyone on the plantation, whether black or white.

# 5

# A Cook and a
# Yardman

If there was anything that the impoverished aristocrats on James Island had in abundance, it was manners. Courtesy to strangers, the tipped hat, the extended hand, deference to elders, first names only after long acquaintance, grace and the set table for every meal. Surface amenities? Perhaps, in part. But practiced over the years they wear grooves that can change character. I remember watching, with little less than awe, an eight-year-old boy enter a room where his parents were entertaining adults, and greet each with outstretched hand.

We had moved, we soon learned, into a rural community not of farmers, but of planters. "Farmers" lived upstate. The men I knew on James Island were planters. They lived on large plantations that bore names laden with history. How did one know that they were planters and not farmers? First, they told you so. They also wore starched collars all day, and a neat hat—never a cap; they rode a horse as they went about their duties—duties that consisted mostly of supervising the Negro workers. They rarely did manual labor, but directed someone else to do it. Nearly all the planting, cultivation, and harvesting was done by the Negro "hands" and the mules. It was not uncommon to see twenty or thirty men and women in a field during the growing season. At noon, there was a short break for the field hands and the planters. The Negroes sat in the hedgerows and ate from a tin pail; the planters rode home to tea and crackers on their front porches. After the hands returned to the fields in the afternoon, the planters returned to their homes for two o'clock dinner.

At six o'clock the plantation bell was rung. Ours at the Bluff, the size of a small church bell, was mounted on a pole by the mule barn. The sound carried clearly across the flat land and was answered soon by the jangle of mule harness, and the bantering talk of the men as they rode bareback from the fields. In planting season a dozen women would follow them, heads wrapped in towels and carrying hoes over their shoulders. I liked this time of day, and I tried to be around the barns and gin house when the men came home. While the plow hands unharnessed the mules, the planter would confer with the Negro field foreman; there would be some jotted notes on who worked that day, and how many tasks were completed, plans laid for tomorrow, and then home to a light supper at 8:30.

There was no confusing such men as these with upstate farmers whom some children, out of earshot of their mothers, called "crackers." As a child, I had always thought that the word "cracker" was strictly a local expression—a word that schoolchildren used when they were angry: "You're just an old cracker!" Its origins were much deeper, I was to learn. The word appears as we have seen in Cecilia Lawton's diary in 1865. She used the term to describe people who were very real to her; after the fall of Savannah she disguised herself as a "cracker."

While Wallace was absent trying to look after his ruined property, Cecilia was boarding at the home of Judge Hobby in Sylvania, a town sixty miles north of Savannah. The city was completely occupied by Sherman's army and no civilians were permitted to enter or leave. Sensing the need for food, the general had ordered that people from the surrounding countryside be allowed to enter the city unmolested to sell their produce.

Two elderly and rather well-to-do women were also staying with Judge Hobby, having been thwarted in their efforts to enter Savannah to rejoin their families. They resolved to take advantage of Sherman's regulation and enter the city disguised as "crackers" selling meat and vegetables. Cecilia reports in her diary she "entered enthusiastically into their plans and was invited to join them."

Judge Hobby supplied a carriage for them and a cart to follow behind with some bacon and other food that Wallace had saved from Sherman's soldiers. The judge also gave them a driver for the cart—a slave whom he recommended as particularly faithful. The ladies spent the first night of the journey in Whiteside, and while they were asleep this "faithful slave" ran away to join the Yankees, stealing the money that Judge Hobby had given him to buy fodder for the mule. "We feared," she writes, "that he would inform the guards of our assumed character and that we should be refused admittance to Savannah. But after much consultation we resolved to proceed and take the risk."

Cecilia then reports in much detail the scenes of carnage and destruction at the roadside. The hundreds of putrifying animals made the ladies' trip barely endurable. She was told that Sherman's troops picked up new horses at each farm or plantation, rode them until they dropped, and then shot them. The bodies of ex-slaves, who Cecilia thinks died of smallpox, littered the roadsides; the "loathsome buzzards were circling everywhere or perched on their prey."

On the way to Savannah, "we practiced the 'Cracker' brogue, and endeavored to dress as became the characters we were assuming—that is, the country people coming to town to trade the products of our farm for fine clothes, etc." But a Union major was suspicious and refused to let the three pass; Cecilia and Mrs. Molenbauer would have to remain with him as hostages. While they waited, Cecilia resisted the flirtatious advances of the major on guard "who showed a disposition to gaze too long and impertinently upon me," while Mrs. Molenbauer "involved him in a heated argument on the subject of slavery and the negro race."

They eventually did receive passes and were allowed to sell their bacon and visit their friends and relatives.

In addition to the Savannah episode, there are many passing comments in Cecilia's diary suggesting that she lived in a three-layered culture—Negroes, crackers (sometimes called farmers), and planters. It will be remembered that she accused the jealous "country crackers" of destroying the beautiful Bennett house on James Island. The distinctions among these groups persisted to my day, although to a much less marked degree.

Whatever the ambiguities of these terms, one thing can be said for certain about a planter—he must have a plantation. I don't know how many acres were required to make a plantation; some were small, compared to the Bluff. Size seems not to have been the critical element. One of the distinguishing characteristics may have been location; the plantation homes of most of my friends were on a waterfront. In the early days this water course, even though usable only at high tide, proved a dependable means of getting to the outside world. The fortunate ones who built their homes on really large bodies of water like the Stono River or Clark's Sound reaped the precious sea breeze in the afternoons. These plantation homes were also spared the vulgarity of the public highway. An avenue led back to the house by the water. The avenue might be picturesquely lined with trees or, more likely, a simple farm road through cultivated fields, but it was yours and you could put a gate across it.

Then there was a certain style that went with being a planter; he must have enough land and other resources to hire Negro labor. There would have to be at least a cook and a yardman, both on a year-round basis. A dozen families or their sons, nephews, or cousins controlled most of the land on James Island. There were, of course, occasional carpenters, shopkeepers, skilled mechanics who came from up-country to live on the island. Although less blessed than planters, they might make a comfortable living with chickens, a garden, and their regular job. Needless to say, they did not hire either a cook or a yardman. The distressing feature of their life style was their too close association with the Negroes. They did not socialize with them, to be sure; they never permitted first names, or use of the front door, but the relationship with the Negroes was simply too close to the horizontal. There wasn't enough gradient. The newcomer's job might also force him to compete with Negroes in the work force, and that was something that a planter did not do. His case would also be weakened by the lack of an avenue, or someone whom he could call cousin—a term that could be used for blood relatives, or for people of equivalent rank. I am happy to report that most of the boys and girls I knew in school could qualify as planters' children.

The system, rank-conscious as it was, and based on shameless exploitation of Negro labor, was nevertheless inflexible in what we could say—the words we could use. We were never allowed to call black people "niggers," never to make comments in their presence about their "loud" or "tacky" clothing, or to ridicule them in any way. True, there were white people who did such things—the crude people from "up-country"; "crackers," perhaps. They were not of our tradition; they had no manners.

The even more stratified society of the antebellum days were brought vividly to mind by the only former slave whom I knew personally. I met "Uncle Peter" Brown during my early days on the Bluff, but it was not until I had read Cecilia Lawton's journal many years later that I fully grasped who he was. For me as a child, he was a kindly old "darkie" with a trimmed beard and a gentle manner who lived at Bennetts, and walked down the pasture road in front of our house on Fridays to buy supplies at the store, and to leave a string of fish for the Bresees. He had a standing order to bring us sea trout or whiting once a week.

His little cottage was at the edge of Charleston harbor on the site of the luxurious Bennett house that Cecilia had described in her diary. It was more commodious and attractive than the average Negro cabin; it had a flower bed by the door and a low, wooden fence around the yard. An improvised wharf that was reached by a plank walkway across the marsh enabled him to take a rowboat into the harbor when he wished to go fishing.

Peter had been a houseman, he told us, a station that set him apart from the other slaves, and permitted him to acquire the polished ways of his masters. There was little of the Gullah element in his talk, and his manner was always deliberate and dignified; he would walk past our house with his hands clasped behind his back, eyes on the ground, giving the impression that he was in deep thought. He talked much more with my father than with me about the old days; he was a good raconteur and was quite aware that he had an interesting story to tell.

Peter often talked of his old master, Wallace, although he never alluded to the beatings he had received in slavery days. The picture of Wallace that emerged from Peter's stories supports the impression I was to gain years later from Cecilia's journal—a man of high energy, hard, and self-serving often to the point of ruthlessness. She wrote that neither her stepmother or father thought Wallace a fit husband for their daughter. Her entries give the details:

My step-mother had taken a violent and unreasoning dislike to Wallace and was using her influence against him, with Papa.

My sister Georgia and brother Aleck were both at my wedding; so that the only absent one of us was sister Rosa.

Papa did not come, being displeased, though I wrote him of the approaching wedding; so that, in no sense, was it a run-away match.

Wallace was a racist to the end, never being able—as Cecilia had written—to relinquish "the spirit of command." A story that I heard many times on James Island tells of his riding to North Charleston on the trolley when a black man entered the car and sat down beside him. Wallace paid no attention to the man, but put a piece of tobacco in his mouth and began slow, systematic chewing. After a few minutes he pressed his revolver into the man's side and spat in his face. He continued to spit on him for the rest of the ride, the black man not daring to move. When Wallace left the car, he is supposed to have said, "That will teach you not to sit by a gentleman."

That story did not originate with Peter, although he did tell of a personal experience with Wallace that contrasts sharply with it.

"I saved Mr. Wallace's life once," he told my father. "It was when we were out fishing on the jetties." The jetties were two chains of room-sized rocks that flanked the channel to Charleston harbor.

The movement of the tides through this man-made narrow channel kept the entrance to the harbor free of silt.

"There was good fishing off the jetties," Peter said, "but you had to know how to take care of yourself because those big rocks were covered with slime. One afternoon Mr. Wallace and I were fishing out there. Mr. Wallace's line got caught and he made a quick move to free it and lost his balance and started sliding. He couldn't stop himself and kept on sliding until he got out of sight in the water. I knew how to swim, but Mr. Wallace didn't. So 'bout the time he came up, I was down there beside him. 'Put your hand on my shoulder,' I say to him, 'but don't choke me.' He grab me pretty hard, but I managed to swim around to a place where we could climb up. He thank me and say, 'You saved my life, Peter.'"

One of Peter's favorite stories was seeing the first shot of the Civil War. His master, Wallace, had given him instructions to be called at 4:00 A.M. This Peter did, and climbing to a cupola on top of the Bennett house, they watched the first shell explode over Fort Sumter.

Peter was no doubt a highly intelligent man, though of course he lacked formal education. Slave owners kept a practiced eye open for bright youths to be trained for house service, or as groomsmen. Such young men became walking proof of the old adage, "nothing succeeds like success," for once taken from the field they began to accumulate personal assets that increased exponentially. Peter was born probably between 1840 and 1845, which means that Winthrop Lawton, who had acquired the plantation in 1813, selected him. Peter shrewdly chose to stay with the Lawtons after freedom and thus escaped the fate of the thousands who wandered away to their death. One is tempted to speculate on how he dealt with the mercurial, driving Wallace during slavery and afterward; he may well have surpassed his master in native intelligence and have seen "in and around and through him" with a clarity that Wallace did not suspect.

It never occurred to me at the time to wonder how this man in his eighties survived in his tiny cottage by the harbor. There was no public welfare or social security, and he had outlived his children. I like to think, but do not know, that his old master's son, Alison, gave him a stipend.


We had not lived in the Cuthbert house very long when John Posey began to take his evening meals with us. A widower of about my father's age, he had come to our plantation to be crop manager and maintenance man. Having a background in railroading and some experience on the prosperous Stono plantation, he was well prepared to take up his duties on the Bluff. He was steeped in Southern ways as my father was in those of the North; they were both keenly observant and good raconteurs.

My mother's menus were not noteworthy, but I do remember our supper as long, leisurely conversation. It is hard to realize now that there was a time when supper did not end with a dash for the TV dials. After dessert, we lingered at the table, or pushed our chairs over by the fire—and talked. Mr. Posey was reluctant to return to his lonesome bachelor quarters, and we certainly did not want him to leave. The men talked and we listened. They vied with each other for the best story of childhood adventures, big storms, long trains, Pennsylvania mountains, North Carolina mountains. Mr. Posey would tell how the great hurricanes of 1911 and 1916 had almost inundated the island, and my father would counter with tales of Pennsylvania blizzards, sub-zero temperatures, and giant snowdrifts.

Those evening talks probably had more to do with my learning to read than anything that happened in school. Mr. Posey might say, as soon as the blessing was over, "I see they had a bad time at the jetties yesterday—a boat smashed up and a man drowned."

"Who was the man? How did it happen?" I was into the table talk in a flash.

"Two of them finally got up on the rocks and were rescued. It's all in the paper today." Or, "The *Lenape* had a fire in its hold when they came into port last night." My eager questions, a few tantalizing details, then as always, "It's all in the paper." I remember being actually angry—I could not read the paper! There would be no answers for my questions on the radio or TV screen. I would find them in the columns of the *News and Courier,* or go without. I learned to read in a hurry.

From Mr. Posey and his experience on the thriving Stono plantation, I heard about the economic history of James Island. The Sea Islands of the South Carolina coast had produced, until the end of World War I, a unique, long-staple cotton that was in much demand in world markets. This coveted fiber made many planters on James Island rich. Then came the boll weevil. With the sudden failure of the long-staple Sea Island cotton because of this destructive insect, planters turned to truck crops. These seemed to have produced alternate years of wealth or bankruptcy, depending on the fluctuations of the Northern markets. Mr. Posey's account of the trials of the planters began to take on meaning for me at this point, because we were raising white potatoes and cucumbers for shipment to Northern cities.

I discovered that anxious days always followed the decision to invest in a crop of potatoes or cucumbers. Corn, sorghum, velvet beans, sweet potatoes were staple crops for our herd of cattle; truck crops were a sideline—a venture that had potential for high profit or complete loss.

Potato harvest happened while we were still in school, but cucumber picking came just after school was dismissed in May. For a few days it mobilized everyone on the plantation. I learned from the supper table conversation the problems of securing baskets, rounding up enough pickers and packers—which meant all the women on the plantation—scheduling the boats to carry to Charleston the mountain of baskets that would accumulate on our wharf, getting them loaded onto freight cars, trying to obtain assurance that the car would not be shunted onto a Virginia siding for two days, the concern over the price in New York on the day the cucumbers were sold, the anxious waiting for a quotation.

Hardy stuff, one might say for a seven- or eight-year-old—the economics of the plantation. But, of course, it was not an abstract discussion; this was basic stuff in the lives of these men, what in the daily round worked and did not work; plans and projections, some honestly expressed anxiety. It was real, not a problem contrived by a screenwriter to be resolved in twenty-two minutes. To a slight degree, but probably far more than our elders suspected, we children shared in the successes and defeats of this absorbing venture. We identified! Our mothers were nutrient and supportive, and the men and fathers were the managers and planners. For good or for ill, that was what we absorbed, without even realizing it.

My father and I were never close, as the expression goes, and I opposed him often, yet there was never any doubt as to his role, or what mine someday would be. We would take care of things. Late on Saturday afternoons when field work was done, and life for the older workers on the plantation had subsided to a restful pace while the young had begun collecting at the store for the evening out, the Bresees dressed up and drove to Charleston. Clean socks, clean knees, a fresh shirt, a tie, and we would be off in the Dodge touring car. A long search for a parking space on or near King Street, then my parents were off to Kerrisons's and we

children to the row of ten-cent stores. Ice cream cones, occasionally a movie, and then the long drive home. Sleep would begin to
subdue us in the back seat soon after we crossed the Wappoo
bridge. My brother and sister would drift off but, oddly, I would
not let myself fall asleep. Headlights of the cars returning from
Folly Beach almost blinded us, but I sat up on the edge of the
back seat and, vicariously, I drove the car home. "Someone *has* to
keep awake and drive," I reasoned. "My father has to be alert.
Suppose *I* had to drive this car home? The least I can do is to keep
awake; it's hardly right for me to drift off." I would sit up in the
back seat blinking at the approaching lights until we reached
home. A lifetime later I can give a fancy psychological name to
that experience; I can also be thankful that fate or happenstance
made moments like that occur.

A custom of our planter friends on James Island that could no
doubt be traced back to "the departed elegance" of their forebears
was Sunday evening tea. My parents loved it. Pennsylvania farmers never took time out for anything that one could call "Tea."
This charming James Island custom certainly had no counterpart
in our Northern farming routine, but we took to it as easily as
birds to air; possibly residual elements of our French ancestors—
long dormant—were awaiting revival by the gentle touch of
Southern manners.

The invitation usually came as we stood under the trees in the
church yard after the sermon, making our farewells for the week.
"Won't you-all come over this evening for tea?" We never refused.

At tea no one was expected to be very hungry. This was almost
a ceremonial meal, but then it couldn't really be called a meal. It
was tea and the perfect time for leisurely talk and a slice of the
treasured fruitcake. Almost every planter's wife on James Island
made a twelve-pound fruitcake just after Thanksgiving. It was an-
nointed periodically with brandy and, served for the first time on

Christmas day, was supposed to last until Easter. Our favorite was the moist dark cake made by Cousin Bertha, who lived at White-house. My mother used her recipe, but, as an ardent teetotaler, could never bring herself to use brandy. "Where in the world would I get the stuff?" (Indeed, in the 1920s, where did anyone get the stuff?) My mother's cake was distinctly inferior, I thought.

My memories of tea were of social life at its best. The hostess did not sit before a silver tea service in a high-ceilinged dining room, and no maid or butler glided in and out of the hallway. We might sit at a table in front of a coal fire in the grate, or on the piazza if it was summertime, and drink from cups that no doubt came from Woolworth's. But there was dignity and courtesy, and the kind of atmosphere that made being on your best behavior seem like fun.

# 6

# *Remember Now Thy Creator*

"As soon as you get settled, I hope you will find a church and involve yourselves so deeply in it that when you leave, people will miss you," wrote my grandfather to my mother, newly arrived on James Island.

There was no Methodist church on James Island—for white people, that is—but there was the James Island Presbyterian Church and the St. James Episcopal Church. I think the Presbyterians got to us first, but as things turned out it would not have mattered. Most of the James Island families were Presbyterian one Sunday and Episcopalian the next. The problem could be stated simply: no one wanted either of these historic churches to close its doors, and there weren't enough planters for both. Loyalty to tradition and community prevailed over doctrinal differences.

There was, indeed, a Presbyterian church complete with deacons and elders, and an Episcopal church with priest and vestry. Both had small Sunday schools. Neither could afford a full-time preacher, the Presbyterian preacher serving also on Wadmalaw Island and the Episcopal priest serving at the Seamen's Home in Charleston.

"Which church today, Mom?"

"The Presbyterian."

"I thought we went there last Sunday."

"We did but this is the fifth Sunday. We go to the Presbyterian church every first, third and fifth Sunday."

"That cheats the Episcopalians. Do they mind?"

"No, because their minister has a service in town on fifth Sundays. Have you studied your Catechism?"

"Yup. Numbers 40 and 41."

"Bring me the book. I'll see if you know them." She read question 40. "What did God at first reveal to men for the rule of his obedience?"

Having just studied the two answers, I was in good form. "The rule which God at first revealed to man for his obedience was the moral law."

"Where is the moral law summarily comprehended?"

"The moral law is summarily comprehended in the Ten Commandments."

My parents both came from Methodist families who could probably have traced their religious lineage back to Francis Asbury had they tried. Methodists did not have a Shorter Catechism, but my parents believed in memorizing religious material and were not concerned about the fine theological distinctions between Methodism and Calvinism. The Catechism seemed to be good basic stuff, so let the kids learn it, was their attitude.

As a child, I found switching churches rather enjoyable. If the word "enjoyable" sounds startling, it should be remembered that the option of nonattendance did not exist in my family. Alternating between the two churches offered a pleasant change. My Sunday school class in the Presbyterian church was held in two short pews at the rear of the church, and in St. James in a nook behind the reed organ.

The Presbyterians stressed the Shorter Catechism. We were issued a tiny brown paperbound booklet that we carried to church every Sunday for several years. We would recite two or three answers every week in Sunday school class, working toward the prize of a New Testament if we could pass the spot questioning by the elders.

The Shorter Catechism got down to basics at once with a stunning first question: "What is the chief end of man?"

It was followed immediately by "What is God?" and "What are God's decrees?"

The chief end of man, I learned, is to "glorify God and to enjoy Him forever." The presence of the word "enjoy" there always puzzled me, for certainly the rest of the Catechism carried little suggestion of enjoying God. The point it made to me in its terse, grim language was that the chief end of man is to obey the stern demands of God, with the clear implication that doing so might not always be enjoyable.

These memorized answers were sometimes useful. Once in college during our innumerable bull sessions on sex, religion, or politics, the most knowledgeable skeptic in our group said, "Sin! The word can mean anything. You can't define it." Somewhere out of the depths it came unbidden: "Sin is any want of conformity unto or transgression of the law of God." The stunned silence in the room fully repaid me for all my childhood labor.

The Episcopalians had their strong points. The rector wanted a choir for each service and gladly accepted children as well as adults. Martha Rivers, the organist and my teacher in public school, knew that my sister and I could sing acceptably, and soon had us outfitted in robes and marching down the aisle behind the crucifer. The rector, although saddled with a small church—actually half a church—leaned toward High Church liturgy and included as many formalities as he could manage with his limited resources. I found the pageantry and movement a pleasant contrast to the plain, colorless Presbyterian service. I liked the divided chancel, the candles, the robes.

To reward the choir and keep up morale, the rector had a charming custom at Christmas time. At the end of the Christmas service he gave each choir member, right down to the youngest, a pound of Norris's chocolates. There is no way by which I could make anyone today comprehend what that pound of chocolates meant to us. First of all, it was a grown-up gift; this was not a box of suckers or candy canes. I remember clearly the Sunday my sister and I brought home two pounds of chocolates.

"Did the preacher"—he was never the rector to my father—"give a box to everyone in the choir?" he asked.

"Yup, everyone. And he had some left over," we said.

"Twenty-five boxes of candy on his salary? He must have a friend in the wholesale business!"

"Seems like one box per family would have been enough," my mother observed. There she went again—my mother and her penchant for moderation. Why couldn't we just revel in candy? Box after box of it! But my mother found it hard to revel in anything.

"It wasn't you folks who did the singing," we reminded her. "*We* did the singing."

The situation put our Sunday school lessons about sharing to the test in a most annoying way. Of course we could and would pass it around, but when do our proprietary rights get recognized? My sister and I had earned this candy, we maintained.

"There were kids singing today who are no older than Kenneth," my sister and I told them. "He's supposed to have such a sweet voice—let him sing next Christmas."

"We'll see," my mother said. "That's a long way off."

The next year our Christmas Sunday came off just as we had planned. Miss Rivers welcomed us with a smile and helped us to adjust our robes. We formed on the church porch, the children leading—including three Bresees. A long procession extended behind us—halfway around the side of the church. There were some new faces in our choir from the Folly Beach area, and I thought I knew the reason for their sudden interest in singing. The service went off without a hitch, including the anthem and the new Christmas responses. While we were removing our robes, the rector came back to the choir room with his arms full of boxes. He handed one to each of us with a big smile and a "Merry Christmas." Just then my mother came by the choir door to hurry us along. She faced three grinning children, each with a box of chocolates. This was too much for my proud, honest mother. This was excessive pay for doing the Lord's work and, besides, the situation looked rigged. "This isn't right. I'm going to see the minister." As she walked away, we could only watch and hope; the matter was no longer in our hands.

"These children do not deserve three boxes," my mother said. "Our family has much more than our share."

"Oh, no, there is a box for everyone who sings in the choir on Christmas Sunday." My mother started to speak. "Now, Mrs. Bresee, you wouldn't want to deny me the pleasure of giving Christmas presents, would you?"

My mother smiled in a sweet, defeated way and turned to us, "I hope you thanked him for his kindness."

In a chorus: "Oh, yes, we have!"

We raced over to the blue Dodge parked under the oak trees, and climbed triumphantly into the rear seat. Three pounds of candy!

Yet as the months passed, we began to think of ourselves as more Presbyterian than Episcopalian. There were two reasons: there was a stronger Sunday school influence in the Presbyterian church, and my father had trouble with the liturgy of the Episcopalians. The formal prayers, the choral responses, "all the fuss about candles and bowing" were a long way from his brand of Methodism. He sang in the Presbyterian choir and was, of course, asked to sing with the Episcopalians. He declined. He wasn't about to get rigged out in a robe and surplice. Particularly distasteful to him was the time when the rector, on special Sundays, turned his back to the congregation and intoned a solo chant.

Our friends, however, switched back and forth easily. My Sunday school teacher, Mrs. King of the Stono plantation and a loyal Presbyterian, would sing "Love Lifted Me" in her church one Sunday, and just as enthusiastically the next Sunday proceed up the aisle of St. James with book held high singing "The Son of God Goes Forth to War."

Perhaps we moved toward the Presbyterians because they did a little more urging and inviting. While the people at St. James were cordial enough, and you always knew that you were welcome, I used to feel that either you were born an Episcopalian or else you might decide in the privacy of your own mind to request to become an Episcopalian. But there would be no unseemly tugging at your sleeve.

# 7

## *By the King's Highway*

The King's Highway cuts across the center of James Island, from Three Trees to the Stono plantation. Someone in Charleston once asked me if it was not "King's Highway," named after a local family. Why did I call it "the King's Highway"? I replied that a dozen of my elders who had spent all of their lives on James Island, and whose knowledge of local history I considered superior to that of anyone in Charleston, had told me that the road was called the King's Highway. I liked the sound of those words, the smack of far-off times they carried—even the hint of some great occasion. There was some debate, I knew, about the origin of the name James Island. No one was quite sure whether the island was named after James I of England, or James, the apostle. Both were illustrious men, however, and either one satisfied me fully. In any event this highway was quite properly named for a great English king and not some early settler. That is why it bears the name the King's Highway.

James Island Grammar School was a little complex of buildings on a historic site. There was the schoolhouse, a set of stables in the rear, two outside toilets back in the pines—one to the left and one to the right—the club house, and the windmill. The two-room school took care of planters' children from grades one through seven. The adjacent Agricultural Hall, which we called the club house, served two prestigious organizations: the Secessionville Chapter of the United Daughters of the Confederacy, and the James Island Agricultural Society. On my arrival there one chilly November morning for my first day of school, I was aware only of the big playground, a solid square schoolhouse, and giant pine trees. At recess I would discover the row of stables behind the school in which stood a half dozen horses harnessed to buggies. Two live oaks, their trunks easily three feet in diameter, stood at one side and shaded a sandy playing area. A windmill, whose creaking we heard most of the day, pumped drinking water.

One day during our first or second year on James Island, our parents had told us to wait at the school until they picked us up on their way home from Charleston.

"Don't try to walk home," they said. "We may be late, but don't leave the schoolyard."

"No need to worry," my brother said. "I'm not walking past Crazy Pigeon's house."

When school was dismissed, some of the children got into waiting cars; the Oswalds and the Cokers trotted off in their little buggies at a brisk pace; and finally Miss Rivers backed out her Model-T and drove away.

The empty schoolyard was ours to do anything with it that we wanted. It was lonesome and challenging at the same time. We could now climb the windmill tower as high as we dared. My brother and I prowled around the stables and even walked out the forbidden path to the "Girls' Toilet" and looked inside. Then back to the club house porch to wait. The club house was a community center building with a second floor that was off-limits to school children. The first floor was a large room that might seat a hundred and was familiar to us children; all we knew about the second floor was that the United Daughters of the Confederacy held meetings there and that we should stay away from it. People called it the U.D.C. Room.

As we sat there, a stray dog emerged from the hedgerow and began sniffing about the schoolyard for pieces of discarded lunch. Mockingbirds wanted the lunch, too, and for the first time in my life I saw birds dive down and attack a dog. The dog was indifferent, however, and went on scrounging. The windmill creaked, and the pines sighed, and we settled down to boredom.

Suddenly my brother called, "Come here a minute!" We ran around the side of the club house. He stood there pointing. The door to the upstairs room was unlocked! Not a soul in the world to watch us—or ever know about it—if we climbed those stairs! We knew that this was forbidden territory, and we were not children who could easily disobey orders.

"I can't see the harm in just going up and looking around," my brother said.

"Do you think they're coming back in a minute? We don't want to get caught up there."

"No, they've all gone home for the day. Someone forgot to lock the door."

We moved cautiously toward the stairs. "You'd better prop open the door," I said. "We don't want to get locked in." Locked in the U.D.C. Room for the night while our parents frantically search the island for us! The thought almost made me sick. We found a stick of wood and put it in the doorway. Then we climbed the zigzagged stairs.

The room we entered seemed like a combination living room and classroom—chairs with writing arms sitting about, a shabby rug on the floor. The same bearded men that we had seen in our classroom were staring down from their picture frames on the wall. Several flags and banners stood by a massive desk. It was the large closet that drew most of our attention. We opened the door cautiously. Guns—perhaps a dozen—were standing in the far end, and barely visible in the dim light were more flags and banners. The guns were obviously old ones—like nothing we had seen the men use for hunting. Gently we unrolled a tattered Confederate flag—I knew it was a Confederate flag because that was the kind we drew in art class—and then we carefully rolled it up again. We tiptoed around the room for a few minutes, enjoying the view from the windows. There was no need to press our luck any further. We went down to the club house porch, locked the door behind us, and assumed a nonchalant air for our parents' arrival.

This little adventure in the U.D.C. Room had no dramatic ending, but it affected me more than I sensed at the time. It was one more impingement of history on my daily life. Living on James Island in my most formative years, I was to be imbued early and permanently with what Tennyson called "a passion for the past." The giant pines on the school ground that I would listen to on long afternoons whispered a message in their sighings of which the concealed flags and muskets in the upstairs room and the rusty cannonball that we kicked around the yard gave only tantalizing hints. Did I not go home each night to a house built in 1747, and on Saturdays play in earthworks that were thrown up to fight the enemy in two wars—the British Redcoats and later the Union forces? Continually there was a sense of great happenings behind me that I must somehow discover, and link to my own life.

A few weeks later we were again waiting at the empty schoolyard for a ride home. This time Fay Coker, a classmate of my sister, was waiting with us. We wandered aimlessly around the school ground and again tried the door to the upstairs room. It was locked. But we thought it was safe to tell Fay of our little exploration of a month ago.

"We sneaked up to the U.D.C. Room a while ago," I said. "The door was unlocked, so we just went up."

"Oh, I've been up there lots of times. My mother belongs to the U.D.C."

"What do they do up there?"

"They meet once a month and talk about the Confederate War—and the veterans. They sometimes serve tea. They all have some ancestor who fought the Yankees—I mean against the North."

"We saw some old flags and banners."

"They were used in the battle of Secessionville. That was fought right here on James Island, you know. That was a decisive victory for the Confederacy." She paused complacently, as if waiting for us to grasp the full meaning of her statement.

"The most important thing up there, my mother says, is the big desk," she continued. "It was made from the foundation of a famous cannon—the cannon that fired on *The Star of the West* when it *tried* to bring supplies to Fort Sumter. That started the War Between the States, you know." She was sounding like a history book again.

"What happened to the cannon?" I asked.

"I don't know, but old Dr. Lebby—he'd be the great-grandfather of Lillie and Hinson and Priestly and, oh, about a dozen people in this school—he got the foundation when he worked down at the Quarantine Station at Fort Johnson—and he made this desk."

"If they just talk at those meetings upstairs and drink tea, what do they do with those guns we saw?"

Fay looked startled. "I never saw any guns."

"They're back in the closet," I said.

Fay thought a moment. "Oh, maybe they're souvenirs." She looked at me a little scornfully. "You don't think those ladies shoot them, do you?"

The discussion ended with the sound of a car horn. I wanted to know more about the guns.

The James Island School served the community, in one capacity or another, both night and day. Not all the night uses occurred inside the buildings. We were not the only ones attracted to the mystic stillness of the pine grove behind the school. Our eyes and ears picked up more than our parents thought they did concerning what were called "goings-on" in the schoolyard. Still, much was unclear. We knew well the possibilities of concealment offered by the hedgerow and the schoolhouse. Then there were the young pines that sheltered the space between the school and the stables. Here was an area carpeted with thick pine straw and quite invisible from the King's Highway.

I don't know what aroused our interest in a serious exploration of this sequestered spot. With so much time on our hands, we did a lot of desultory wandering before and after school. We knew every bush, tree, bird's nest, and hiding place. We might just have stumbled on it—lying there in the pine straw one Monday morning, moist, crumpled, utterly mysterious. Someone poked it with a stick. We stood there puzzled, but at the same time remembering the subdued conversations of our elders. Someone had seen cars drive into the schoolyard at night. The pine straw was obviously disturbed by car tracks. One thing was becoming certain—this little white curled-up object was connected with the people who parked here on weekends! Then someone advanced the first plausible hypothesis. The most convincing evidence was the shape. We made the mental leap—so *that* was what they used it for! But we had strayed beyond our depth. One of the boys hooked it on the end of a stick and vaulted it over the stable. Miss Rivers would be ringing the bell in a minute. With instinctive discretion we decided not to tell the girls.

Monday mornings now took on new interest. We could not put Satan behind us so easily. Anytime we cared to look, we could find fresh evidence. We began to speculate about the people who invaded our schoolyard every week—probably "city folks" or "that new crowd at Folly Beach." But one day a boy called us aside to tell us a story with calculated deliberation.

"We were all in our car going down to Seaside last night. Daddy was driving; oh, it was about eight o'clock and we were just riding along—you know, just riding along—and there was this car in front of us, and we followed it down the road. The sand was deep so we couldn't pass. We knew whose car it was, and we figured it would turn into their avenue in a minute, anyhow. But it didn't! It kept right on going and turned into the schoolyard. We saw it go back behind the schoolhouse."

He paused for effect. "It was . . ." He named a James Island boy who attended the College of Charleston and was a member of our church! It was unthinkable—someone right in our midst. I had watched him pass his Catechism test! Alerted now, we picked up more of our parents' undercover remarks.

"It's perfectly disgusting!"

"Enough cars there for a convention!"

"Even if we put chains across, we couldn't keep them out."

Can children go to school anywhere without anxiety? I came across a photograph the other day that my parents had taken of the three of us packed into the little gig, hitched to Bessie, ready to depart for school. "The simple rural life at its best. Not a care in the world." Indeed! I lived in daily fear that the field of broom grass around the school would catch fire again. And if it happened, it would be set by the same boys—none of whom appeared to have learned from experience.

Half the pupils might arrive at the school ground in the morning before the teachers did; we had nothing to do but stand around and look for mischief. Playground duty for teachers was unheard of then. Most of the boys carried matches, not for smoking, but to light little fires of pine straw to keep us warm until we went inside. Where was the best pine straw? Under the trees near the broom grass field. I never had any doubt of my ability to manage such a fire safely, but there was that dumb bunch from the Folly Road. They would even start a little grass fire, let it blaze a moment, and then all pounce on it to put it out. One day they did not succeed. It suddenly whipped away to another clump of grass, a breeze came up, and it was off into the field. This field enclosed two sides of the school ground, coming close to the stables in the rear. By now everyone was scared. Red flames were swirling into the tall grass, absorbing it in big gulps. The teachers ran toward us with brooms. What could a broom do against a six-foot flame? The big boys ran around to the stables to try to keep the flames from the building. I unhitched Bessie and turned her over to my sister in the middle of the playground. Several Negro men appeared from nowhere carrying hoes. They set to work on the edge of the fire nearest the school. I suppose the schoolhouse was not in danger as long as we watched for flying sparks. We could do little with the fire but let it roar and keep it from igniting the stables. After a while the fire burned off in another direction, and we gathered in the middle of the yard, each trying to explain how his unique act of bravery had saved the school. The teacher rang the bell and the matter ended. Ended, that is, for all but me. Each year as the pine needles fell, and as we regularly made our little fires, I would experience a nervous twist in my stomach, and wish that the starting bell would call us inside.

A second worry for us was Crazy Pigeon. Driving to school was great fun during those first days of September, except when we were suddenly exposed to the madness of this woman. She was a danger that we had not anticipated. Could we get safely past her house in the gig? Crazy Pigeon was a demented black woman who ran after all passersby, screaming and gesticulating. For the children in James Island Grammar School, she possessed a witchlike quality.

The first day of the new school year was over. Bessie had stood docilely in the stable all day, and we were ready for our first journey home. We loaded our new books and lunch boxes into the floor of the gig, and the three of us packed ourselves onto the small seat. We drove down the King's Highway for a quarter of a mile to where the Bluff road slanted off to our left. Over the summer we had almost forgotten Crazy Pigeon. Besides, when we saw her last spring we were riding in a car. Somehow, we had not aroused her when we had driven by this morning. Our gig rounded the curve onto the Bluff road and Bessie settled into her leisurely walk. My brother was driving, and my sister was fiddling with her new pencil box. In a few minutes the hedgerow on the right side of the road gave way to the hard-packed dooryard of Crazy Pigeon's house. For the first time I was anxious about our position, but said nothing. Maybe we would be lucky. But suddenly the door of the cabin flew open. A disheveled woman in a baggy dress stood in the doorway staring at us. Then with a big cry, half shout, half wail, she jumped to the ground and started running toward us. The chickens in the dooryard scattered like leaves. Kenneth shouted at Bessie and flailed her with the reins. She lurched forward while we hung onto the iron rail. I sneaked a quick look at the panting woman laboring in the sand behind us. What was the look in her disordered eyes? Was it anger or hate or fear? She was now gasping heavily and began reaching out for the railing at our backs. Gladys, half sobbing, screamed, "Get away! Get away from us!" Staring up at my sister, the crazed woman began repeating in a half moan, "Oh Jedus! Oh Jedus! Oh Jedus!"

Kenneth had now gotten Bessie into a loping gallop, and Crazy Pigeon, struggling in the deep sand, was rapidly losing her wind. She was now being followed by a stream of brothers, sisters, aunts, cousins—we never knew which—who had emerged from the house and were giving chase. In a moment they reached her and took her firmly by the arm. She submitted easily. They did not shout at her or strike her; these measures had no doubt failed years before. They simply led her back to the house.

I never knew her family name or those of any of the people who rushed after her each time we passed the house. I never learned how this pitiful creature got her name. The children in James Island School all called her Crazy Pigeon, and we all told tales of narrowly escaping her clutches. We were always relieved to see people standing in the yard as we approached, for they always restrained her. When no one was outside we would whip Bessie into a gallop and look neither to left or right as we swept by.

Crazy Pigeon's house was located on a triangular piece of land that was owned exclusively by Negroes. This triangle was known as the Cocked Hat. Its inhabitants, not attached to any plantation, lived from their little gardens and from what they could earn as transient workers. I was to learn years later that the owners of this tract steadfastly refused to sell any piece of it to white people. To this day the triangle is owned exclusively by Negroes. I do not remember wondering how this family dealt with the tragedy in their household. Did neighbors stop in and help on bad days? I do not know. No planter, certainly, felt any responsibility for people living in the Cocked Hat.

We were spectators only of this misery. Seriously ill and disturbed as she was, she was probably never seen by a physician. Crazy Pigeon was a real person in the sense that she was corporeal and assaulted our sensibilities daily. Yet in another sense she was not real. She had no name, no birthday, no family, no past, no future. She simple "was." I never wondered what might become of her. There was no evidence, moreover, that anyone in my world gave a passing thought to Crazy Pigeon's sad life.

# 8

# *For Southern Rights, Hurrah*

We were getting nicely settled into the James Island way of life when my brother asked at the supper table one evening, "Mom, what's the U.D.C.?"

"It means United Daughters of the Confederacy."

"What do they do?"

"Oh, I don't know. Patriotic things, I suppose. Their fathers and grandfathers fought in the Civil War—on the Southern side—and these ladies don't want people to forget them. Why do you ask?"

"Some ladies came to school today to talk about it. There's going to be some kind of important meeting."

My older sister jumped into the discussion with all the authority of a bright girl reciting in class.

"I know what it's all about. We're going to celebrate General Robert E. Lee's birthday. He was the commanding general of the Confederate army, and one of the world's greatest generals. We're going to sing some Confederate songs and recite some poems and have a lot of important people over from town. Some of the men were soldiers in the Confederate army when they were young. They're going to tell all about their experiences and about the battle of Secessionville."

"Where'd you get all that?" my brother asked, trying not to look impressed.

"Miss Rivers told us all about it in history class today. Are you coming, Mother? Everyone is supposed to."

"We'll see," my mother replied.

When my ninety-two-year-old great-grandmother Mary heard that our family was moving to Charleston, South Carolina, she had remarked sadly, "Why must they go to the hotbed of the rebellion?" In the Pennsylvania of those days there were only lingering memories of the great conflict, but on James Island, where the first shot of the Civil War was fired, the coals still glowed.

Robert E. Lee would have two charming and spirited women planning his birthday celebration. Martha Rivers, principal of the James Island Grammar School and my teacher, would nowadays be called the coordinator. Her father, Captain Elias Rivers of Centerville plantation, had been an officer in the Confederate army; her mother's family had lived on the Secessionville plantation, scene of a bitter battle—and of a Southern victory. Then there was Mrs. St. John Alison Lawton of our plantation, who had recently been elected national regent of the United Daughters of the Confederacy. Descended from an aristocratic Virginia family and married into the prestigious Lawton family of South Carolina, she possessed impeccable connections for this high office. The families of both of these women had brought their plantations back into productivity and had moved comfortably into the twentieth century, but in each woman lay the inherited memory of injuries that would not stay continuously subdued.

General Robert E. Lee's birthday on January 19 offered the perfect occasion to relive it all, and "how fitting that the children from James Island's historic plantations should participate." Earthen breastworks still zigzagged the fields and roadsides, and at the eastern end of the island stood Fort Johnson where the first shot of the Civil War was fired. If a military victory could not be celebrated, there were heroic deeds and honorable deaths; there was the Southern Cause—a victory of the spirit that must not be forgotten. We began immediately after Christmas holidays to learn the old songs, the most impressive to me being, "Hurrah for the bonnie blue flag that bears a single star. First came South Carolina and then came Georgia, too . . ."—followed by the whole secession chronology.

We Bresees made so many blunders in those days—my sister leading off with a question about the Civil War. "Gladys," Martha Rivers said to her, "we call that the Confederate War, or you may say the War Between the States. It was not a civil war."

It was my turn next when I was asked to play a march while "the little room" marched into "the big room" for the celebration. After only a year of piano lessons, my military music repertoire was not extensive, but my mother found a piece that she enjoyed, and thought "easy to march by." In a simplified version it would do perfectly, she thought. So at the time appointed I sturdily pounded out "The Battle Hymn of the Republic." Luckily, that was rehearsal day. Before I went home that afternoon, Martha Rivers called me aside and said, "It takes so short a time for the little room to march in that I don't think we'll use any music. You played it very well, tell your parents. Would you like to read a short poem for us?"

"Yes, Ma'am. It's O.K. with me."

"Here is the 'Ode' by a famous Charleston poet named Henry Timrod. Have your mother help you with it and we'll practice again tomorrow."

Shortly after the lunch break, long black cars from Charleston began rolling into the schoolyard. Since the day was mild, we children were to wait outside until the guests had been seated. A Negro chauffeur got out of the first car and assisted a white-haired man, who limped badly, up the steps into the school.

"He's one of the veterans," someone beside me whispered. "I'll bet some Yankee shot him in the foot."

I decided that this remark was not made for my benefit and did not respond. Several more black cars came in rapid succession, each containing old men who made it up the steps to the school only by the aid of canes and helpers. Soon the parents of some of my friends, in more modest cars, began to arrive.

"Are your father and mother coming?" a girl beside me asked. "Mine are. They think old Mr. Welch is wonderful."

"My folks don't know much about Lee and the Confederacy," I said. "We fought on the Northern side, you know."

"They could come today if they wanted to—and just watch. My father and mother think you folks are nice Yankees."

We entered the school to see a row of veterans and U.D.C. officials facing us from the front of the room. Mrs. St. John Alison Lawton, wearing a wide scarlet ribbon diagonally across her substantial bosom, presided. She gave my sister and me a warm smile of recognition, causing the children sitting nearby to stare at us in amazement. She was, Martha Rivers had told us earnestly, the *national* president of the United Daughters of the Confederacy. She was usually off to meetings in Richmond or Atlanta, and it was wonderful that she was taking part *here*. I remember being attracted to her from the moment I had seen her on the plantation. She had the strong, expressive voice of an actress, and a rich laugh that radiated poise and self-assurance.

In all I must have participated in at least five celebrations of Lee's birthday. They were similar in style, except that I saw fewer white-haired veterans each year, and Mrs. Lawton, when not president, came as a guest. Two veterans stand out in my memory— one I liked and the other I did not. They attended most of the programs and usually gave the same speeches each year. The white-haired man whom I did not like had a long, lean, and intense face. Time had not mellowed him as it had the other veteran who spoke. He described with a fierce relish the acts of suffering and bravery that he had seen at the battle of Secessionville. One almost got the impression that he was glad there had been an enemy to fight. And always we were admonished never to forget—especially not to forget the atrocities of Sherman's march. The marauding soldiers shot all farm animals they did not wish to take with them, poured molasses and turpentine on the corn meal, shot any man, woman, or child who got in the way, and torched all the buildings. All this I had heard many times in history class. Of course, he said, we all knew of the recent horrors of the war in Europe. In the 1920s the memory of World War I was still fresh. He told of the Germans' heinous treatment of the Belgians as the Germans marched through that helpless country, destroying and torturing as they went. Did we not realize, he said, that Hindenburg had learned many of his vile practices from General Sherman and modeled his march after Sherman's march through the Confederate States? Even to my little fifth-grade mind, that did not ring true, and at the conclusion of the speech I refused to clap. I sat with my hands clasped on the desk, trying to look as disapproving as I could. "I believe that man notices that I'm not clapping," I thought.

My brother and sister did clap, and I argued with them all the way home from school. I told them at the supper table that they should have known better.

"I don't think the Germans ever bothered to study the Civil—the War Between the States, I mean. I think he made up a lot of that stuff just to impress us," I said.

"I clapped because it was polite," my sister put in. "I don't really care what he said. He's probably just a mixed-up old man. If it made him feel good, I'm glad I clapped."

"It didn't make me feel good and I hope he saw me."

"You mean you sat there and didn't clap?" my father said.

"Nope. I just sat there and looked at him." It was one of the rare times when I think my father was genuinely pleased with what I did, for I learned later that he told this story to several of his Northern relatives.

The other veteran, a Mr. Welch, had seen the first shot fired, and had been with Lee at Appomattox. Moreover, he had stood by the gunner on Fort Moultrie whose shot had brought down the Stars and Stripes over Fort Sumter. I can remember his calm, almost academic voice. "I will not say that I was unmoved when I saw the Stars and Stripes fall to the ground. I was not filled with elation, because I sensed, even in the excitement of the moment, the significance of what we had done." On retiring from the military, he had risen to a high position in Charleston business circles, and was greatly admired throughout his long life.

The recitations and songs of the children broke, from time to time, the succession of speeches. Our attention was often called to the portraits of Confederate generals that hung on the wall, Stonewall Jackson, Pierre Gustave Toutant Beauregard, defender of Charleston, Wade Hampton, Robert E. Lee—the only generals who existed for us in James Island Grammar School. Brave men they were, who fought against enormous odds and were never defeated—reverses they had experienced, perhaps, but never defeat.

The mood of the afternoon changed after Mr. Welch's speech. His calm, almost scholarly account of the war somehow tucked events back into their appropriate niches in history. I do not think we could have sung "Hurrah for the Bonnie Blue Flag" quite as lustily as we had two hours earlier. By three o'clock in the afternoon a bit of the Confederacy had slipped away from us.

The closing remarks were quite contemporary—appreciation to

Miss Rivers, and for the efforts of the children. We were back in the twentieth century. "And to conclude this memorable day," I can hear Mrs. Lawton's hearty voice, "let us all rise and pledge allegiance to the flag, and sing a stanza of our national anthem."

> I pledge allegiance to the flag . . .
> one nation, indivisible . . . .

The stricken flag at Fort Sumter was flying again over the "land of the free and the home of the brave."

At supper time my father and mother listened with great interest as we recounted the day's events. We even sang for them a stanza of the new song we had learned about the bonnie blue flag that bears a single star.

"And then you pledged allegiance to the flag?" my father asked. We nodded.

"At least they ended it right," he said.

But there was a fact in my father's background that he kept from us during the early years on James Island. Our family, too, I was to learn, could report great deeds in the Civil War. My father's father falsified his age, enlisted in a New York regiment at sixteen, fought for three years, and was wounded. At age seventeen, he captured six Confederate soldiers in the battle of Spotsylvania Court House and marched them to his company commander. For this feat he was awarded the Congressional Medal of Honor. My father probably knew that no small Yankee boy could be trusted on a Southern school ground with that information when arguments heated up.

"My grandfather, single-handed, captured six rebels without even firing a gun! Brave guys, Confederate soldiers, . . ."

# 9

# Offspring of the Moon

It is fashionable for writers on child rearing to state that a growing youngster should be given clear limits—within which he must learn to operate. No doubt they are right. All children, I suppose, must learn, however grudgingly, to accept territorial limits, as well as those imposed by the clock and the seasons.

For us on James Island there was another limit—fixed and unyielding—the movement of the tides in the creeks and inlets. The weather is a wavering and unpredictable parameter, the seasons give even weeks of leeway, but the tides give nothing.

Maybe I shouldn't write about the tides. All the thoughts and feelings they have evoked must have long ago been set on paper—or canvas, or in a score of music. Is there anything new to say? My English teacher had this in mind, no doubt, when she advised us not to write about the moon. What more can be said about the moon? I should have replied, "I have not yet spoken." I see now that she was wrong. She should not have restrained me, and she does not now. An authentic experience is not made less dear because the words are trite. James Island Creek, a small boy sitting at the end of a dilapidated wharf—and the great marsh slowly filling. It was I and no other who sat there and for the first time felt this offspring of the moon rise and softly brush my feet. No

account of my boyhood can omit such banalities as springtime, sunrise and sunset, first love—and the tides.

A commonplace to those who live at the sea's edge, the tides are a never-ending wonder to millions who live inland. The tides were a mystery to ancient man and have in our time yielded up only part of their mystery to the probing of science. Students of the ocean continue to ask hard questions about this vast movement of water, and they continue to get inadequate answers. The bulge of waters toward the moon, along with the turning of the earth, helps to explain the tides in a general way, but a clear look at the actual behavior of water in a particular sound or inlet raises questions that the bulge does not fully explain. People who live alongside one of the arms of the ocean, as we did, people whose livelihood is intimately related to the flooding and ebbing of tidal waters, soon work out their own timetables, and order their daily routine accordingly.

The coast of South Carolina in the Charleston area is actually a series of sunken river mouths. The ocean lies to the east, then the long, narrow, barrier islands with their beaches and sand dunes; behind them are the stream-threaded marshlands. Still further westward is dry ground—dark, fertile soil bearing water oaks and pine trees. Was this the mainland? At first sight one was never sure. If a tidal stream had slipped behind this tillable land to link itself with another, then this was a Sea Island—Wadmalaw, Edisto, Johns Island, James Island. A few miles further west, however, the streams would no longer turn back upon themselves, the influence of the ocean and the tides would cease, and one had found the mainland. Collectively, this was called the low country.

As we children knew by the tides when to put down our nets and lines for shrimp and fish, so did my father and his friends watch in autumn for tides that would take them marsh hen hunting. In late autumn when the creek was approaching flood stage, two men in a flat-bottomed boat would push out over the marsh. One sat in the rear and poled or paddled; the other crouched in the front with a shotgun.

The game they sought was a small shorebird that is a member of the rail family, a furtive bird more often heard than seen. According to Forbush and May's *Natural History of the Birds,* "It slips about the dense growth of salt marsh plants, invisible to the prying eye of the bird student, now and then giving utterance to its harsh cackling cry . . . first from one direction and then another . . . as if rails were children in a game of blindman's buff. If there is a particularly high tide, they are sometimes forced out of their shelter in the tall vegetation, and may be seen running over floating 'thatch' or drifting around on a bit of flotsam, waiting for the waters to subside."

The species that men hunted in the marshlands of James Island is called Wayne's clapper rail, described as inhabiting the chain of low islands along the coast of South Carolina and Georgia, and the broad tidal marshes that lie between them and the mainland.

"It is a prolific bird, often raising two broods totaling two dozen offspring annually, but it has many enemies to contend with, the two worst being man, who hunts the bird tirelessly, and the occasional high tides which, driven by an easterly storm, may flood the breeding grounds and destroy all the eggs or young over a large area of marshlands." These odd-looking birds with their excessively long beaks and almost tail-less rumps might easily have been named the "bobtailed" something or other.

I never went on these boat trips across the flooded marsh, because I could not manage a double-barreled shotgun; neither was I strong enough to pole the boat. It was good news for us children to hear that "Dad is going marsh hen hunting" because it meant a great platter of fried marsh hens for dinner. Dr. Ted Bowers, our family physician, was often the guest for these expeditions. The men would row across the main channel of the creek and then assume the hunting positions as they entered the marsh. Though they might soon be lost to our sight, we could stand on the wharf and hear the muffled shots of their double-barreled guns. They would stay out until dark, or until the tide had turned.

Perhaps the hunting on morning "highs" was not good, for I always seem to remember the men returning just at nightfall. We would try to be at the wharf when they pulled in. The bottom of the boat would be covered with birds grotesquely tossed about in a blood-stained heap. Then the counting and the dividing of the hunt. The men, wet and chilled, were full of exuberant talk about near-misses and the shot that brought down two. We would often carry home over twenty marsh hens.

Curious, indeed, that the tides should bring two modes of destruction to this shy bird. A high tide in spring brought the death of eggs and fledglings; a high tide in autumn brought men with guns gliding over the marshlands in flat-bottomed boats.

During my childhood, fishing, swimming, boating, crabbing,

shrimping—and, to some extent, travel—were all a function of the tides. One learned never to ask for permission to fish or to swim when the ebb tide was in full flow. The swirling water around the wharf supports and the brown angry whirlpools as it raced to the harbor told us plainly to stay on shore. This was a place for power boats, which we did not have, and not for flailing arms and oars.

The gentle flood tide brings us to action. One can read in the newspaper when the moment of low tide is to occur at the Custom House Wharf. The paper does not, however, tell us when the moment will come far back on James Island Creek. But by lying prone on the wharf that juts out into the creek, and staring at the mud below us, we can detect the magic moment. A crab hole is covered, an oyster shell disappears. The tide is turning and the options are opening fast! Now we can push a boat off and go fishing. Or if an adult remains within shouting distance, we might row out to the sandbar and swim. Conversely, when the tide is moving toward full flood, and we are swimming, if fatigue does not stop us, the ebbing tide will. A patch of fresh mud appears at the shoreline; the brown whirlpools are beginning to form. Resigned and uncomplaining, we leave the water. Not father or mother, but the tide has spoken.

On other days, with a little planning, we could persuade our parents to drive us to Stiles Point plantation where, as the tide approached flood stage, we might swim in Charleston harbor itself. But it was more fun to swim at the Bluff, and we liked it best if the tide was high in late afternoon. James Island Creek then was a lake a mile across, with the water lapping at the piling a foot below the wharf floor.

In addition to James Island Creek—which in many parts of the world would be called a river—there were other streams and inlets that backed in around the larger plantations. There was Wolfpit Run, an arm of James Island Creek, that wandered in behind Centerville plantation almost to Camp Road. Another tributary of James Island Creek, known as Simpson's Creek, meandered far into the island, split in two, and caused us to cross the "first" and "second" bridges on our way to school—bridges that we scarcely noticed until spring tides. The south side of the island had Clark's Sound, which provided a waterfront for several plantations.

Back at the Bluff there was Mill Creek, flowing into Charleston harbor and separating the Cuthbert and Bennett areas of the plantation. Wallace Lawton's grandfather had put a causeway and dam across this stream, and used the impounded water to operate a little mill. We traveled this causeway whenever we visited the site of the Big House out at the harbor's edge.

There was also an inlet behind the Cuthbert house, nameless as far as I can determine, a marshy low place into which tide water from the Ashley River backed daily. Bordered by water oaks, pasture land, and thickets of cassena bushes, this area was alternately a shallow three-acre pond or marshland through which a small stream wandered. This stream, threading its way through two or three acres of marsh and low ground, was a James Island Creek in miniature. The Bresees called this area "the Tide" and the name stuck.

In retrospect, I wonder whether a more exciting or mysterious place for children could be designed by experts. First of all, it was safe. Except during spring tides, the water was never over a foot deep. If we called over our shoulders that we were going down to the Tide to play, our parents did not worry. All the fascinating and lovely phenomena of the tide lands were here in miniature. There were fiddler crabs and blue crabs, baby shrimp and minnows; there were herons and rails in the marsh grass and mockingbirds and cardinals and loggerhead shrikes in the bordering thickets. Most important of all, there was moving water. With a wooden Tinkertoy set we could make a water wheel that would turn slowly in the ebbing tide. I shall never know how many sticks and balls from our Tinkertoy set drifted away from us into Charleston harbor. We would think, "Maybe now they are in the Atlantic Ocean." Our little fleets would float for a quarter of a mile on the ebb tide. One day we would make a dam of mud to retain the high water, and the next day erect a barrier against the incoming tide. Our engineering efforts would grow more and more frantic—to be abruptly replaced by the new and exquisite pleasure of watching our structure slowly crumble in the rushing water.

The tide always won.

## *10*

# *Grits and Butts-Meat*

The term "plantation store" has for me, now that I am grown up, a dark, exploitive connotation. When as a ten-year-old I used to visit it with five cents to spend it had no such meaning. It was a place where Negroes of all ages gathered—a place of good talk, and of good things to eat. Whether the store exploited the workers on the plantation, I do not know for sure; it probably did. It was supposed to make money, and there was no competition near enough to matter.

Its location, from my point of view, was superb. Standing at the edge of the Negro section, it was the first important building one came to on the road leading to the Bluff, and it formed the shore-end of the wharf. No one came by land or water without passing the store. It sold groceries, tobacco, and candy on credit, to the limit of the employee's weekly earnings. There was an ell-shaped counter around two sides of the room, and a large bin for oats and corn in one corner. During busy hours our customers had to struggle to find a seat on this bin. The short side of the ell was for the icebox which held Try-Me—the local soft drink—butts-meat, bologna, and lard. Grits, sugar, rice, crackers, and canned food ran down the long side of the ell as far as "dry goods." This department consisted of overalls, denim pants, a few bolts of cloth and thread. There was also a glass-enclosed case for Hershey bars and penny candy. Squares of sticky flypaper lay about on the counter and spirals of it hung from the ceiling. By modern standards the store was shabby, unkempt, and certainly had too many flies; its customers were poorly dressed Negroes who, when they were not barefooted, wore shoes that never had laces.

The store and our wharf were actually a unit. The store was overshadowed by three large water oaks whose huge, bark-covered roots had long ago been exposed by erosion, and now stood several feet above the sand. On hot days, these roots, the store porch, and the wharf provided excellent lounging places, for they offered an unobstructed view of the sandy road along the creek that led into the plantation. Like most James Island buildings, the store had a wide porch—this one without railings—weathered and sloping. To modern eyes the scene shouted deprivation. If a team of social workers traveling through the low country had come upon this shabby building, shimmering in the summer heat, where half a dozen scantily dressed Negroes sat idly swinging their legs from the edge of the porch and two small mud-spattered boys were trying to catch shrimp with a burlap net or wading through muck to get a boat offshore, they would certainly have paused for a consultation: Something Must Be Done!

My brother and I were the two white boys—absorbed with our gear and working against the tide. We caught shrimp on the flood tide, played elsewhere on the ebb, and fished on the rising low tide. There was mud to our knees and there were cuts in our feet from oyster shells buried in the black ooze, but we felt good about ourselves. We knew those boys on the store porch and we liked them. They were waiting for the return of the *Palmetto,* or some other excitement that probably wouldn't happen.

Surely this was the poverty-stricken South buying its grits and butts-meat from the company store. The store was probably never perceived by the blacks then as exploitive, for it met needs that could be satisfied elsewhere only by miles of travel—on foot. As long as the plantation produced crops, a closed group of workers could have jobs. The few dollars earned in the fields, supplemented by vegetables from a tiny garden and seafood from the creeks and inlets, were enough to maintain life in a temperate climate.

The little society on the Bluff bore similarities to a feudal estate that in retrospect I now find disturbing. But back then my brother and I recognized no social problems, at least none that we could do anything about. We rarely entered the little two-room cabins to which the customers of our store carried their purchases. Each house consisted of a combination living room-kitchen, and one sleeping room. The little cabins had no windows or screens; at night, winter and summer, the solid blinds and doors were closed up tight—a reasonable move since there were no screens. Curiously enough, these decrepit houses often appeared neat. One might observe cynically that it is not difficult to keep a table and a few straight-backed chairs neat. There was no litter around most of the cabins; the Negro section was quite unlike the pockets of rural poverty that one sees today. The reason may have been that there were no tin cans, cardboard boxes, or broken-down automobiles to be disposed of, because these people had none of these things. A diet of grits, sweet potatoes, and butts-meat makes little garbage. Cooking was done on the hearth, over a wood fire.

How they kept these little fires burning on cold mornings was one of their problems that I entered into personally. Their only fuel was a little pile of dry branches stacked outside the door—a little pile that was always running out. The Negroes in those days faced far more serious problems, I suppose, than lack of fuel. There was inadequate medical care, insufficient clothing, illiteracy—to name a few—but none of them hurt me like a cold cabin, and a fire that wouldn't burn. Perhaps it was because Ned

kept a supply of chopped wood always at hand in our back yard.
I had seen how hard it was to cut and split enough wood to cook
a meal. The little coal bin behind our house always had enough
coal for the fireplace grates.

The Negroes were allowed to roam the plantation in search of
fire wood, but could not cut down live trees without permission.
It was the women's task to collect into bundles any dry wood they
could find lying on the ground and carry it home on their heads.
The search for fallen trees and dead branches might take them
more than a mile from their cabins. The long route home wound
through the pasture lands in front of our house, and we often saw
the women struggling under heavy loads. On the scale of poverty
and misery, this scene was somewhere near the bottom for me.
Shivering in front of my own fireplace on a December morning, I
would watch these women, wrapped in their husbands' oversized
coats and sweaters and balancing a bundle of sticks on their heads,
coming home across the fields to a cabin that had no fire. I would
think of them when we sang the carol "Good King Wenceslas":

> . . . the frost was cruel
> When a poor man came in sight
> Gathering winter fuel.

I cannot say that anyone ran forth like the good King Wenceslas
to offer help, saying:

> Yonder peasant, who is he?
> What and where his dwelling? . . .
> Bring me flesh and bring me wine,
> Bring me pine logs hither . . .

Neither I nor anyone else on James Island followed the example
of the good king. I was genuinely distressed, but there was relief
available; James Island planters of those days had thought-

patterns already prepared for me, and I used them. "Why do they always wait until the coldest morning of the year to search for wood? Why don't they plan better—make their lives more systematic? It's their nature, no doubt, to live from hand to mouth."

We liked to be in the store when Uncle Peter made his Friday afternoon visit. He was probably our most distinguished-looking customer—black or white—a man with a large well-shaped head who always wore a straw hat, never a cap as most Negroes did. We knew he was old because he had been a slave, yet he was more erect in bearing than many of the younger men. Everyone, of course, was younger than Uncle Peter, and deferential to him in the little ways that age can command—a little less noise when he entered the store, greetings that were more extended and proper, a polite effort at conversation. He bought the usual staples, grits, rice, butts-meat, flour. The storekeeper or my father would usually say, "Let me send these over to your house this afternoon on the milk truck," or, "Leave these with us, Peter. One of our boys will be driving out your way this afternoon." It didn't seem right that an old man in his eighties should have to carry this big a load for a mile and a half.

One Friday afternoon in midsummer, Uncle Peter came across the pasture toward our house carrying a string of fish in one hand and steadying a gun on his shoulder with the other. He came to the back porch, knocked, and asked for my father, who happened to be home that afternoon.

"Well, well, what do we have here?" my father exclaimed.

"This is for you, Mr. Breezy," he said, removing the gun from his shoulder. "I want you to have this. I'm getting old and no telling what will happen to it when I die."

"Did you ever use it, Peter?"

"No, I bought it in a pawn shop about fifty years ago."

"How old do you think it is?"

"It's an old Springfield like they used in the war. It's a muzzle loader," he said, pointing to the ramrod. "Slaves weren't allowed to keep weapons," he continued, "but I always liked old guns. Mr. Wallace had a lot of 'em in the big house. All gone when they burned Bennetts. So when I had earned a little money after freedom I went to the city and bought this."

My father and Uncle Peter had early formed a warm friendship. A mutual respect had developed between them as the new young boss at the Bluff listened eagerly to Peter's firsthand accounts of slavery, the war, and early days on the plantation. Peter, like most people who live alone, welcomed an appreciative audience during his weekly visits to the store. He knew that this newcomer to the island would treasure an antique gun; my father accepted it as an expression of genuine friendship, and told Peter so. They examined the old piece carefully, conversed a while longer about the war—repeating old questions and old answers—until my father said, "I've got to ride out to the dry pasture to check on a cow that has freshened. You stay here and rest a bit, Peter."

"I thank you, suh," he replied. Then he sat himself slowly and carefully on the edge of the back porch and gazed out across the cornfield.

Meantime my brother and I had gotten kitchen knives and a pail of water and had begun to scale and clean the fish down by the woodpile. After he had rested a few minutes, Peter walked down to watch us. The harbor was at our backs as we worked, and Peter stood facing us, his eyes on the city skyline. I could not know or care then of his memories of eighty years of serving the Lawtons; he was just a kindly old man, watching us clean fish.

"There was once a road where you boys are setting," he said, "that ran clear back to the water there." We looked behind us, out across the cornfield to the Ashley River.

"How old were you then?" one of us asked.

"Just a young fellow. I've seen a lot of changes on this plantation."

"Were you born here?"

"Yes, I've always belonged to the Lawtons. We lived around Beaufort for a few years when the Northern soldiers took over the island. Then we come back here and I stayed on after freedom. That road to the water," he continued, "was lined on both sides with a row of osage orange trees. People used to go back and forth to a little wharf by the marsh. Boats could load up there on high tide, and cross over to the city."

He looked at the Cuthbert house behind him. "That house has seen a lot of things happen. Some good—a lot of 'em bad. I was sure glad when Mr. Lawton decided to fix that house up for you folks."

"Did it look pretty awful?" I asked.

"When we come back to this plantation from refugeeing, it look so bad we didn't even come near it. After a while Mr. Wallace say he will never have enough money to build another big house like Bennetts, an' he say he might as well fix it up. After we work on it awhile, it look pretty good, and he an' Miss Cecilia move in."

He glanced down at the sea trout I was gutting. "That's fish roe you see there, boy. Fish eggs—the best part of the fish. You want to keep them, and have your mammy fry 'em in a little butter."

I don't remember how our conversation ended. We went on cleaning fish and Peter must have walked back across the fields to his little cabin at Bennetts.

In the same manner, he quietly walked out of our lives. Word came to us some time later that his strength was ebbing and that he could no longer take a rowboat into the harbor. Since the kind of fish he liked could not be caught from a wharf, the Friday visits to our house ceased. The weekly trip down the pasture road to the store to buy supplies also stopped without anyone really noticing. Then one evening after supper, my father said calmly, "Uncle Peter died today."

It was hard for me to make Peter's description of the tree-lined road leading back to the harbor seem real. It would have cut directly across a rich cornfield called "the farm." I used to stand at my window at night and try to picture men and mule carts moving to and from the wharf on the Ashley River. I reasoned that the road must have reached the water's edge at a break in the hedgerow where there was a patch of broom grass and a little grove of wild persimmons. Sometimes when we wanted to play in a spot where we thought no one could find us, we would go there and build a tiny fire and sit looking at the city. Could that have been the place, I now wonder, where Wallace Lawton's canal boat the *Stark Naked* began its trip across the Ashley so many years ago?

"Hanging out at the store," as my parents called it when they wanted us to come home, provided the best opportunity there was on the Bluff to keep track of what was going on in the outside world because, as I have said, the store was the first building to be encountered by anyone entering the plantation complex. The road that led into the Bluff was a "dead end" road; visitors unaware of this fact came into the store to ask directions or to buy gasoline from the pump by the edge of the porch. There were regular visitors, too. Two young salesmen from the wholesale grocery firms in the city came once a week with jokes and snappy talk; the driver of the gasoline truck was always sociable. The "bread man" from Condon's bakery, a swarthy, voluble, ex-marine who had fought in Panama, came twice a week. After filling the bread case he paused for a half-hour social call that included soft drinks and cinnamon rolls "all around." Frequently he left a supply of yesterday's cakes and cookies, which we could either give to the white families or sell at half-price to the hands.

Since the only telephone on the plantation was fastened to the wall of the store, we could hear the out-going half of all conversations. Without the distraction of a steady background of recorded music, radio, or television, we found listening to our elders' conversation easy, indeed—talk of crops, boats, fertilizers, mules, broken machinery, and sick cows.

I heard much talk about sick cows, for my father called the veterinarian often; on a plantation such as ours, there was almost a daily health problem among the cows and mules. Because of his natural aptitude, training, and experience, my father could diagnose and treat many of the problems himself. He was a highly perceptive observer of a cow's eyes, eating habits, energy level, and general demeanor; we used to say that he knew when a cow didn't feel good before the cow did.

Still, my father often called both the local and state veterinarian. Tuberculosis, a disease common among cattle in those days, afflicted many of our cows. The disease is transmissible to humans through milk, against which pasteurization is a protection, though not a perfect one. In order to eradicate the disease, the state offered a small indemnity to the owner for any "reactor." The Bluff lost cattle each year to tuberculosis, but with each annual test new cases were discovered. The situation caused my father much concern, not only because of the financial loss, but because of the presence of active tuberculosis bacteria on the plantation.

The disease was a source of much anxiety to parents because it afflicted children and young adults in particular. In school, we learned that a generous supply of fresh air was imperative if we were to avoid contracting tuberculosis; the health authorities told us that we should sleep with a window open every night—preferably two. My mother, always alert to scientific advances, promptly made us comply with the recommendation—much to the annoyance of my father who suggested that she furnish us ropes for holding the bed covers down.

At school we also learned that a sanitarium for the care of "TB patients" was to be built up the Ashley River near Summerville; it, too, would emphasize the fresh air treatment, with patients sleeping all night on screened porches under the pines. The schoolchildren of Charleston County were invited to enter a contest for naming the new center. Many of the James Island children, including the Bresees, sent in suggestions, but they did not win. The first prize went to a girl who submitted the simple and appealing name "Pine Haven."

Tuberculosis was to vex us throughout our stay on James Island. Two of my school friends would live at Pine Haven, and my brother would contract the disease before we returned to the North. Colds that "hung on," a persistent chest cough, a rundown look—these all sent parents hurrying to the doctor. While the white families sought diagnosis and treatment, the black people who crowded our little store and locked themselves up in their cabins at night probably had their share of infection, but the health of black people was rarely discussed. Or were they largely spared the disease because they consumed no milk? I do not know.

The most exciting event of the week occurred in the store—the payoff on Friday nights. Three white men were required to conduct the transactions properly—my father, John Posey, the crop manager, and Mr. Knight, the storekeeper. Soon after the quitting bell in the evening the workers began to gather at the store. A

Rochester Burner kerosene lamp hung above the counter, illuminating the record book over which the men leaned, but giving scant light to the dark figures crowding the room. My position at this event was always behind the counter. There was no place for a small boy among those pushing, bantering men.

Gross earnings for the week, less fifty cents house rental, less the sum on the store's books, was the rule. Unless there was a fine.

John Posey begins calling names. "Henry Washington—$7.20." There are no secrets on payday. The cash register clangs and my father counts out the money.

"James Middleton . . ."

"Isaac Brown . . ."

And so on down the list. Occasionally there was a protest. "I didn't buy *dat* much at dis stoh."

He is shown the book. "No, maybe you didn't, but Wilhelmina did," puts in Mr. Knight. There is no recourse. He leaves grumbling.

A crap game starts in the corner on top of the oats bin. They play softly and a shield of watchers stands close around them so that the white men won't notice.

There are also fines to be paid. This, too, is announced for all to hear.

"Joe Davis—eight dollars, one dollar fine. You broke a hoe handle last week."

"Mistuh Posey, dat handle was too weak. He brake himself."

The crowd in the store goes silent.

"No, it didn't. Cain Aiken saw you get mad and break it."

He is handed seven dollars. "Better watch your step next week, Joe, if you want to work on this plantation."

Joe backs away from the counter, muttering. But the judgment sticks.

When the last person had picked up his money, my father closed the book. The men began to converse again as they lounged on the oats bin and around the soft drink counter, digging their hands deeply into their pockets to finger the few bills and coins they had received. The feel of money brought conviviality, and a desire to savor some of the luxuries of life. Mr. Knight did a land-office business in Try-Me and milk biscuits. A quarter pound of bologna, eaten slowly and meditatively with a bottle of cream soda, was a treat that a man could have only once a week—and only on payday.

With the payroll business out of the way, Kenneth and I could now start the Victrola and sell penny candy. The store had the only phonograph on the Bluff. A transient white worker had owned it, but could not take it with him when he caught a ride to Savannah. He never returned. He left a stack of records ranging from "Star of the Sea" and "Whispering Hope" to "Yes, Sir, That's My Baby," "Show Me the Way to Go Home," and "Black Bottom." On Friday nights the thin, nasal music from the wind-up Victrola gave a carnival-like touch to the milling, sweaty little crowd in the store. We tried to accommodate requests. The sweet-sad "Star of the Sea" was surprisingly popular. But "Yes, Sir, That's My Baby" and "Black Bottom" brought out the electricity in the crowd. Keeping the Victrola wound and a fresh needle in place occupied the most of one person's time.

Our candy business is strictly cash, because the men know that Kenneth and I are not allowed to make entries in the record book. As I wait behind the candy counter for customers, a smiling black face leans into the glass in front of me.

"Hello, Bill," I say. "Whatcha gonna have?" I recognize him as

Bill Gardner, Flora's nephew. I like him. He lives with his uncle, Ned; he is a man about twenty, a good field hand, honest, affable, and poor.

"Clyde, how 'bout two Mary Janes and one cent wut o' Banana Wonduhs." The grown men rarely buy five-cent candy bars; the variety and quantity of penny candy are what they want most. Mr. Knight is glad enough to have help on Friday nights; we perform a real service. He is kept busy all evening with groceries—cutting and weighing butts-meat and bologna, scooping rice and grits into five-pound bags—and can hardly afford to spend time on penny candy. Besides, our father has given us permission to be here, and that is final.

Bill is still peering into the candy counter. "Den . . . I tink," he continues thoughtfully, "I gonna play Pick-a-Pink."

I place before him on the counter a broad, shallow box of chocolate-covered mints that sell for a penny each. In the center of the box are a dozen candy bars to be given as prizes to the lucky winners. He studies the little circles intently. "I tink I take . . . dis one." He picks it up and breaks the chocolate covering. The center is white. "Oh—oh, no luck." If the center had been pink, he could have selected a free candy bar. He counts the coins in his pocket.

"One mo' time." He bends over the tray of chocolates.

Just then I notice that the Victrola is running down. The ladies singing "Whispering Hope" are becoming deeper and deeper contraltos, and will soon quit in a guttural groan. I can't wind it now and leave someone alone with Pick-a-Pink. A voice in the room calls out pleasantly, "Bettah wind dat ting up, Clyde." I decide to stay with my customer and let the music die.

Finally Bill chooses a mint and takes a quick bite. Center: pink! "Dat's de bes' luck I had dis week." He picks up the candy bar and pushes two pennies across the counter. I replace the Pick-a-Pink box in the case, rush to the Victrola, and give the crank a few brisk turns. The ladies revive, come promptly up to pitch, and finish their song.

We are now back to normal. Men and girls from neighboring plantations are collecting on the porch and wharf; I hear scuffling, and protest, and girls' laughter, and more scuffling. The four men who are playing cards on the oats bin have attracted a respectful circle of onlookers. This is a casual game among friends; no one is tense or anxious. The players may be exchanging coins, but no need to worry as long as the constable doesn't ride up. Someone would recognize his horse long before he arrived and sound the alarm; plenty of time for corrective action.

I heard that one afternoon the constable *did* appear and threaten to make arrests for gambling. My father and all the other white men on the plantation, pleased with the state of our race relations, saw no point in disturbing men and boys who were betting pennies on their afternoon off. My father is said to have called the constable aside and told him angrily that he had better spend his time hunting real crime on James Island—"I can give you some leads, but you don't want them"—and to stop throwing his weight around among a few boys who weren't hurting anyone. The next time he wanted to come hunting on the Bluff he could bring a warrant. Or words to that effect; that was how the story came down to me.

When business was light, Kenneth and I could sit on the oats bin. One day we watched some boys play a card game that they called "Kaseena." They seemed not to mind our peering at their hands of cards; we knew enough about such games not to talk. After a while one of them said, "Wanna play? We teach you. Dis is easy." It was, indeed, easy and in a few minutes Kenneth and I were playing "Kaseena." After the boys left we found some cards in the store that nobody claimed and carried them home so that my sister could learn to play, too.

For the next several weeks our favorite pastime was to stretch out on the parlor rug and play "Kaseena." My mother's family had never permitted cards in their house, and I did not realize then what a departure from her way of life the scene before her must have presented. Soon we became adept at shuffling the deck and calling out the names of cards—three of spades, queen of hearts, jack of diamonds—a language that my mother could scarcely understand. One thousand miles from home, she was able to consider the matter of cards with some objectivity. We were having a good time, we were not quarreling, we were out of her hair. It looked like a harmless game.

But our days of flirting with worldliness were numbered. One summer afternoon Mrs. Dorothy Ravenel of Oyster Point stopped for a visit. She spoke to us as my mother greeted her and came over to where we were sprawled on the floor playing "Kaseena." We had not been on James Island long enough to rise when an adult approached us, and hold out our hand. She looked down at the cards for a moment. "What are you playing? Oh, I see. You're playing Casino. That's so much fun! Are you using pennies, or matches?"

"How do you do that?" we asked.

She gave an airy little laugh. "Now, I'm not about to give you children lessons in gambling! You-all go on playing just as you are. Have fun."

She and my mother moved into the dining room, but I could hear them still talking. "Tom and I used to play Casino for hours soon after we were married. He had played it a lot when he was in the Navy, and was awfully good at it. I hate to tell you how much he won . . ." Their voices passed out of hearing.

So this card game that her children were playing was really Casino! Even my sheltered, rural mother had heard about casinos; they were places of dissipation, where the Prince of Wales spent so much time.

We received no lecture on the evils of cards; they just disappeared. The next morning we couldn't find them. "Your father and I have decided that you should play something else."

"But why not? This game is a lot of fun."

"We've decided not to have playing cards in the house anymore."

"Is it because Mrs. Ravenel thought we were gambling?"

"She didn't say any such thing. Your father and I have just decided."

"What can we play?"

"Well, there is Parcheesi and dominoes. Flinch and Old Maid are card games." The rolling dice of Parcheesi somehow did not disturb the Methodist conscience.

We protested that these were "kids' games," and not half as much fun as "Kaseena"; we lost. Playing cards never appeared in our house again.

Another near-iniquitous diversion, for which the store was partially to blame, had to do with a song.

> Show me the way to go home. I'm tired and I wanna go to bed.
> I had a li'l drink about an hour ago, and it went right to my head.

This thoroughly singable song, with its lilting—not to say lurching—melody, caught our fancy. We sang it everywhere.

> Wherever I may roam—over land or sea or foam—
> You will always hear me singing this song—show me the way to go
> home.

Coming from the lips of her young children these words were too much for my mother. Orders were given—never were we to sing it again.

"But everybody does," we argued.

"Well, they shouldn't. It's an awful song."

"We aren't going to get drunk, Mom."

"I hope not—but you shouldn't even sing about it."

But that ingratiating melody would not leave us. Sometimes, if we felt the mood was right, and if we were standing near the front door where a quick escape was possible, we would run out of the house, singing in our most debauched voice, "Had a li'l drink about an hour ago and it went right to my head."

The sociability of Friday night spilled over into Saturday. Field work often kept our customers busy in the mornings, but after midday the store again became a center for black people who lived in our part of the island. My brother and I could still sell candy if we chose. We enjoyed the flippant exchanges, the easy-going mood, the horseplay, and we used any excuse we could devise to spend Saturday afternoon at the store.

One day a young man whom I had never seen before came into the store hesitatingly, and then moved toward my father.

"Is you Mr. Brezee, suh?"

"That's right. What's on your mind?"

"My name Bill Heyward, suh. I wuk down at Seaside fo' Mr. Bee." He fidgeted nervously. "I tink I be dere 'bout fo' yeah."

"What kind of work did you do?"

"I wuk in de feel most ob de time. I take ca'h ob de mules at night." Then he came to the point. "I don' like Seaside no mo'. I want to wuk at de Bluff."

"Did you have any trouble with Mr. Bee?"

"No, suh. Mistuh Bee a good man. I don' like his feel man, but we ain't had no trouble, suh." He hesitated again. "You know Agnes Scott, Mistuh Brezee. She wuk heah. We gwine git married and she tink you need mo' hand."

"Well, let me think about it," my father said.

"Thank you, suh. I come back—mebbe Monday?"

My father's "think about it" is a delaying tactic, with a specific purpose in mind. He will telephone Mr. Bee at Seaside, a fellow planter and a fellow member of the James Island Agricultural Society. This will be no ordinary checking of references, no request for Mr. Bee's opinion. Bill Heyward will move to the Bluff only with Mr. Bee's consent. In the fraternity of planters, one must do as one would be done by.

Bill Heyward was lucky; with the blessing of both my father and Mr. Bee, he came to the Bluff.

## II

# How Are You,
# General Beauregard?

A half forgotten fort on James Island was the scene of one of the sharpest local engagements of the Civil War. No marker commemorates the battle of Secessionville or Fort Lamar. No plaque lists the almost 900 men who were killed, wounded or captured there.—The Charleston *News and Courier,* 1964

But there *was* a monument to the battle of Secessionville. I was present when it was dedicated, along with all the pupils of James Island School. I remember the event clearly. We gathered in a respectful circle around a veiled monument that stood about five feet high. There were prayers, and someone read Henry Timrod's "Ode." The James Island School sang "Hurrah for the Bonnie Blue Flag," and a squad of young men from The Citadel, smartly dressed in gray uniforms and milk-white gloves, came to attention, raised their rifles and fired a salute. Julie Seabrook, a great-granddaughter of a Secessionville planter, approached the monument and carefully cut a cord. The silk fell away and we saw the granite face for the first time. There was a burst of applause, and then silence. A cadet played taps.

This Stone Marks the Site of
the Battle of Secessionville
June 16, 1862
Erected by Secessionville Chapter
U.D.C. 1924

Then there was a speech by a man whose name I can't remember. He said that the battle of Secessionville was a major victory for the South. This did not surprise me, because the South won all the battles that I had studied in Simms's *History of South Carolina*. This little book never informed me, and neither did anyone else, that the Union forces overran James Island and that most of the planters fled inland. It did tell me that the North was soundly defeated in the hotly fought battle of Secessionville. And after that? I assumed that the Yankees withdrew and went back to their Northern cities.

As we stood on the little of neck of land at Secessionville and looked out over the waters of Clark's Sound, I knew that Federal gunboats had once plied these rivers and inlets that laced the southern side of James Island, but I never suspected that any soldier had dared to step ashore. Where the Union forces came from and how they got to this battlefield were never discussed. It never occurred to me that Union forces might have been there all the while.

There were approximately twenty-five named fortifications or batteries, as they were called, on James Island during the Civil War. A line of a half-dozen earthworks stretched across the eastern third of the island to hold back an enemy that might enter through Clark's Sound, a small bay with enough arms and inlets to provide waterfronts for a half-dozen plantations, including Secessionville. At this strategic site an additional stronger battery, Fort Lamar, was erected. Still another group bordered the wide, navigable Stono River to the south. There were also batteries on the Bluff and Bennetts that faced northward on the harbor. There was really no effective way to defend the deeply scalloped borders of the Sea Islands against landing parties; one could only hope to block off segments of the island itself.

Charleston, the hotbed of the rebellion, was regarded by the

North as a prime target, long in need of a sound trouncing. The battle of Secessionville, fought on June 16, 1862, was the first major effort to capture Charleston. The second came a year later when a sea attack failed to get through the harbor defenses. The third and most sustained effort was a series of land assaults on Battery Wagner on Morris Island, resulting in the ultimate occupation of that island. From there shells could be lobbed into Fort Sumter and the city of Charleston.

Folly Island and Morris Island! These two barrier islands were our favorite recreation spots during our stay in South Carolina. They both protected James Island from the surf. Folly Island, to the south, was separated from Morris Island by a small river known as Lighthouse Creek that flowed from the broad marshlands into the Atlantic Ocean. Morris Island lighthouse stood by this creek; at the northern end of the island was Cumming's Point, with its fortifications that overlooked the harbor entrance. As children we were totally unaware of the struggles these sandy islands had seen.

We loved Folly Beach with its ten miles of sand—so hard that you could barely dent it with your heel—and the warm surf. We came to Folly Island only for picnics and swimming parties, and then only on sunny days—always planning to arrive at low tide when the famous beach was exposed. A trip to Morris Island was an excursion of the first order. One needed a good-sized launch, a pilot who knew the channels that meandered through the marsh, a picnic lunch of huge proportions, a swimsuit, and a long day. First, a chat with the lighthouse keeper and his family who lived the year round in a big two-storied house, then a climb up the 175-foot cylinder of brick, and at last a little walk around the promenade deck at the top. While we drank in the view of the ocean, the breaking surf that extended as far as we could see, and the miles of marshland to the west, the lighthouse keeper told of the hurricanes he had "sat out" at the top of the tower. The light must be kept burning! Then off over the sand dunes for a picnic and a swim in the ocean.

Our little party had swum alone on the vast beach. In late afternoon, sticky with dried salt water and hungry, we were back at the launch. Then the homeward trip winding through the marsh and skirting the edge of the harbor; we lounged on top of the cabin, munched sandwiches, turned our faces into the breeze, and reflected on the day's pleasures. By dusk we were cruising into James Island Creek.

If anyone that day showed me the site of Battery Wagner and the fort at Cumming's Point, I was too young and uncaring to pay much attention to Civil War history. Charleston was defended by a string of forts extending north and south of the harbor entrance. To the north were batteries on Sullivan's Island, and Hog Island. Almost in the channel stood Fort Sumter; closer to the city were Castle Pinkney and Fort Ripley, located on tiny islands. Many land-based guns would have to be silenced before an enemy ship could enter the harbor.

The southern approaches to Charleston harbor were guarded by a major fortification, Battery Wagner, on Morris Island. Further south, across a small inlet, was Folly Island and south of that lay Kiawah, both of them long narrow barrier islands that Union forces used as landing sites and staging areas. The North was just as determined to capture Battery Wagner as the South was to hold it. When direct attacks from the sea failed, the Union forces planned a land assault by working up from Folly Island. Using this route, they finally landed a substantial force on the southern end of Morris Island.

There was consternation in Charleston when the news reached the city. "The fall of Wagner," said one Charleston newspaper, "ends in the fall of Charleston." An appeal went out from the governor for planters to donate their slaves to work on the fortifications. Every able-bodied male slave between the ages of sixteen and sixty was conscripted and rushed to Morris Island. In the early summer of 1863 a thousand men were laboring behind the sand dunes of that barrier island.

While the conscripted slaves were toiling on Morris Island to fortify their masters' positions, in Boston an idealistic young reformer named Robert Gould Shaw was training the 55th Massachusetts. This regiment of 600 Negroes—many of whom had earlier been sold on the block—would return to the South to fight for the release of their brothers. Assigned to the Charleston area, they would be pitted against the troops of General Pierre G. T. Beauregard. The 55th was to land on undefended Kiawah Island and move northward until they engaged the enemy at Battery Wagner on Morris Island. From Kiawah, they crossed first to Folly Island, where they labored heroically in the July heat of 1863, making zigzag trenches as they inched their way toward the Confederate positions. Next they crossed Morris Island Inlet and worked their way up the island. On the night of July 18, the 55th Massachusetts Volunteers attacked Battery Wagner. Their popular commander, Col. Shaw, led his troops personally against the fort. He reached the top of the parapet, and while he stood alone, waving his men forward, he was shot. His body tumbled to a ditch at the base of the fort among his dead and dying troops. Promised reinforcements did not come, and the 55th—with all commissioned officers dead—fought on until nearly the entire regiment was destroyed. Battery Wagner would eventually fall to the Union forces, but not until a thousand men had been buried in the sands of Morris Island.

I was to cross the trail of the 55th Massachusetts Volunteers once again, many years after I had left James Island. While visiting Charleston I was invited to join an excursion to then-remote Kiawah, where we would spend the day swimming, collecting sea shells, and reveling in the solitude. Here also one needed a good launch, and a pilot who knew the shifting channels at both high and low water.

We tied up at a crumbling wharf, and then sprayed ourselves with mite repellant while Tom Welch set off to find Sam and his two-wheeled mule cart. Southern chivalry would prevail here also for, while there was no good reason that all of us could not walk the half mile to the beach, the women and girls were to ride in the cart; all males would travel afoot. Sam had provided some overturned crates to serve as seats for his passengers in the weather-beaten cart; the men helped six or seven women and girls squeeze into his little box on wheels, and we were off. Sam, walking beside his mule, led the little procession down a sandy trail into the brush, the big, ill-fitted cart wheels swaying crazily left and right as the mule settled down to heavy pulling. Suddenly, the thicket of bushes and small trees gave way, and the sky and sea burst upon us.

Lonely, sun-swept—the surf crashing incessantly on a beach that glimmered away in the mist and spume as far as eye could see—it was the epitome of all the barrier islands. No one lived on the island now, but in an earlier day a planter named Vanderhorst had grown Sea Island cotton on the fields behind the sand dunes. Like all who had raised that precious long-staple fiber on the Atlantic coast, he was driven from business by the boll weevil. His large, three-storied brick and cypress house, now abandoned, stood as a sad reminder of his prosperous days on this fragile island. The land passed to other hands, there was no upkeep of the house, and an occasional summer party such as ours, could now wander through the empty rooms at will. We made our way into the entrance hall and stood looking and listening. We then moved into what had been the dining room. We spoke hardly at all, and then, in quiet voices. The past closed in thickly around us. We were drawn to the heavy wallpaper—imported from France, we speculated—that was peeling from the wall by the fireplace. But here on the white plaster was handwriting! In a neat open script was written:

> The 55th Massachusetts Volunteers.
> How are you, General Beauregard?
> Veritas vincit

Cumming's Point is the northernmost tip of Morris Island and overlooks the harbor entrance. The Confederates, sensing its strategic importance, had installed cannon and manned it with a group of young Citadel cadets. This obscure outpost goes down in history as the site from which the first shot of the Civil War was fired. *The Star of the West*, a passenger ship taken from the New

Orleans run, had been selected to carry supplies and men to the beleaguered Fort Sumter. The hope in Washington was that a passenger vessel might slip into the harbor and not arouse the guns on Moultrie and James Island. The plan failed, because the boys on Cumming's Point saw the boat first.

The date was January 9, 1861, and a fortnight after passage of the ordinance of secession. The young cadets on Cumming's Point were no doubt trigger-happy, and certainly not in the mood to let a Union ship pass. They fired their twenty-four-pounder; cannonballs struck the ship in several places and rolled around on the deck. No one was injured because the commander had concealed all his troops below. *The Star of the West* turned and steamed out to sea.

For reasons that were always obscure to me, this was not considered the first shot of the Civil War. This dubious honor fell to a shot fired from James Island's Fort Johnson. The Cumming's Point attack on *The Star of the West,* while it was hostile, did not result immediately in warfare. The cannons on James Island, that morning of April 12, were aimed at a fort and evoked a return fire. President Lincoln then called for volunteers and the war was on.

People who like to set up historic markers should be thankful, I suppose, that the first shot can be traced back to durable James Island. For now, a century later, the sand dunes and beaches called Morris Island have yielded to the pounding surf. Erosion has taken away all but a few shreds of the island; the proud Morris Lighthouse, once a half mile back from the shoreline, is now standing in the open sea, abandoned and listing badly. The sands of Morris Island—on which hundreds of men toiled through the summer of 1863 to shape their crude batteries and breastworks, and on which a thousand died in combat—are now adrift on the ocean's floor.

That day in 1924 when I was eight years old, the Secessionville battlefield on James Island was also yielding to erosion. The winds and rains were slowly reducing Fort Lamar to a mound overgrown with smilax and cassena bushes. Planters were removing hedgerows and remains of old breastworks as they enlarged their fields to accommodate the new tractor. The Secessionville Chapter of the United Daughters of the Confederacy clearly had work to do. They could not stop the "march of progress," but they could erect a monument to their heroic forebears.

Only snatches of this story were known to me as I stood that afternoon before the newly unveiled monument on Secessionville plantation. It was hard to be serious. I could not visualize a battle—try as I might—with cardinals and mockingbirds darting in the bushes, the children standing close beside me, the talk and laughter of workers floating in from a distant field. Angry men, shouting, running and falling, lunging with bayonets, shooting to kill—I could not make the picture fit on these quiet fields. There had been a battle, because everyone said so. I certainly did not see it as part of a grand strategy, or an effort to punish Charleston for leading the rebellion. To me on that bright afternoon the issue was simple; the Confederates were fighting to defend their homes and their honor against an attacker—and they won.

## 12

# *Ned, We Need You*

Our yardman Ned was a man of a hundred duties and almost as many bosses. It was always:

"Have you seen Ned? Tell him to come down to the gin house."

"Tell Ned to take the cart to the cucumber shed."

"Tell Ned they are getting low on wood at the big house."

"Where's Ned?"

"Ned will you . . . ?"

I always thought of Ned as well past middle age. There was gray in his whiskers and he walked heavily. His work could best be described as lending a hand, errands, and "checking on things." He had no stated hours of work—and certainly no stated time off. Since his cabin was only a stone's throw from the wharf, he was perpetually on call. One of his heaviest duties was to have a supply of chopped stove wood always available at the houses of the white families on the plantation. It was probably the hardest physical labor that he did, and he rested often.

Ned was in charge of John and the cart. John was the name of the mule. The pickup truck on the plantation was the two-wheeled mule cart. Unfortunately, too much weight fell upon John's back, but what the cart lost there it gained in maneuverability. John could turn a cart around "on a dime," and back it into the most improbable locations. He remained in harness all day long, but when not working he was allowed to drift about the dairy buildings to crop grass where he could find it. I could not imagine life on the Bluff without Ned and his cart being continuously available.

If you needed Ned quickly, the best place to look for him was "down at the gin house." Cotton was no longer raised on the Bluff, and the gin house had slowly been transformed into an all-purpose building. Much of the ground floor became stalls for a dozen mules. The huge one-cylinder gasoline engine that once turned the cotton gin was used to grind corn for the cows. To get the engine started Ned required a helper working with him on the six-foot flywheels. It would wheeze and emit a sharp explosion as the two men climbed the spokes of the big wheel. Sometimes the engine backfired and spun in reverse. I used to wonder what would happen if Ned and his helper didn't get their arms and legs out of the way fast enough when the wheel took off. The rest of the engine room had been expanded into a tool and general repair shop; you could get almost anything fixed at the gin house.

I suspect that one of the first tasks that Ned did for the Bresees was to kill and dress a goose for the new family arriving from the North. A flock of about thirty large, white geese roamed the plantation and supplied Christmas and Thanksgiving dinners for the white families. In earlier days the geese may have been kept for their feathers, but during our stay they were turned loose to drift aimlessly over the fields like errant ships in full sail. We left them alone. When they were angry or "broody"—which was most of the time—a female goose would suddenly leave the ranks and dart at us in a terrifying manner, wings spread and hissing like a steam engine. I never understood the pictures in children's books of little girls calmly escorting a flock of geese. They scared us to death. In the late afternoon they gathered at the gin house to make a few tentative splashes in the creek and await Ned's handout of corn; we always stayed clear of them.

A service that Ned performed daily for us was to harness Bessie to the two-wheeled gig and bring her to our door at eight o'clock in the morning. James Island Grammar School was two miles away—walking distance perhaps, but not for planters' children. My father found Bessie somewhere—a graying, gentle horse that could rarely be induced to go faster than a walk, and an old two-wheeled gig. The men at the gin house painted the gig red and put a back rail around the seat, so that the three of us crowded on the small seat would now be safe in case Bessie were to start up suddenly. But no one really expected Bessie to do anything suddenly.

Bessie required about half an hour to haul the gig to James Island School. We tied her in a stall behind the schoolhouse and left her to doze until mid-afternoon. The trip home was always brisk and pleasant; Bessie almost trotted. Back at the Bluff we gave her a drink at the mule trough and tied her up at the gin house to wait for Ned.

Ned also dressed our fish and killed chickens for us. Every Friday afternoon Uncle Peter brought a string of whiting or sea trout to our house, and after a few lessons I too learned to scale and dress them. Chickens were a little more complicated. We had a flock of about thirty mongrel chickens for which a small coop had been built to house them at night. By day they roamed the fields and laid eggs in the coop only when they felt like it, seeming to prefer bushes or the woodpile. We were always on the prowl for hidden nests. If we found a nest of eight or ten eggs, however, there was no way of telling how old they were. They must be broken immediately, and if they passed the freshness test my mother used them at once in what was for us a rarity—angel food cake.

One morning my mother came to the door and called to my brother and me in the back yard.

"Where's your father?"

"Gone somewhere."

"You're so helpful. Do you know where Ned is?"

"He went to Thirty-six with a cart."

"Oh, dear. I wanted one of them to kill a chicken. The veterinarian is going to be here for supper and I can't have salmon again."

"Do you want us to buy something at the store for you?"

"No, all they have is butts-meat."

"Do you want us to catch a chicken—just in case they get back?" We always enjoyed running one down.

"Yes, maybe you should have it ready. Try to find one that isn't laying. And I don't want a rooster, because we'll never get him tender."

"Oh, sure," we said. We knew that we must try to find a large hen that did not have a floppy red comb—a combination not always available. Normally we would capture chickens after dark, when they are approachable. That being out of the question now, we would have to run one down. We had done it before and enjoyed the chase. We were discovering what a sportsman told me years later—that a determined man can chase down almost any wild animal. We would start casually, almost cruelly, so confident were we of the outcome. If she was one of the slimmer birds—like one bearing black minorca genes—she would take off in full flight over the inlet. No matter, no hurry, she would have to alight sometime, and we would be there. At length we would fall upon her crouched in a thicket, gasping for breath.

This time we began searching the woodpile and the bushes that bordered the tide. The dozen chickens cackling in the coop we knew could not qualify. We finally settled on a speckled hen of moderate size that had no comb; we chased her down in the usual manner and put her under a basket by the back porch.

Still no Ned and no father. An idea was beginning to form. I had watched the beheading so often that I thought I could do it. I never saw the execution as cruel or painful, because my father had always said, "We do it quick with a sharp ax and they never know what hit 'em." Maybe I should try; maybe it was my duty to help. It was a job that men did, a little messy at times but necessary, and with Ned and my father absent the responsibility fell on the oldest son. Besides, I wanted to prove to myself and everyone else that I could kill a chicken.

I said to Kenneth, "I think I could chop her head off if I had to."

"Well, you don't have to. Mom can open a can of salmon again."

I could see that he shared none of my primitive instincts to provide for the family. We hung around the back porch waiting for something to happen. Kenneth found some leftover cat food and pushed it through the cracks in the basket.

"Her last meal," he said. But the chicken ignored it.

Finally, I said, "I can handle the ax if Kenneth will hold her feet."

My mother, who had come to the door, said, "Well that might work. Would you help him?"

"Nope. I think we ought to wait for Ned or Dad."

"I had so hoped to have a chicken," my mother said. "Well, I suppose I can hold her legs if Kenneth is afraid to."

This was too much for my brother. "Oh, I can if I have to."

We carried the hen down to the woodpile and found a good-sized log. Kenneth held her legs, closed his eyes, and looked behind him. Just as I lifted the ax, he lost his nerve and loosened his grip. Too late! My ax was on its way down. It took off the first half of the chicken's bill. We both panicked and Kenneth completely released the chicken. Fully rested now, she took off into the air with a strange squawk, and flew into the bushes down by the tide. We raced after her and brought her back to the woodpile.

Ashamed of our loss of nerve, we finished the job in silence. We carried her to the back porch where my mother had a pail of scalding water ready.

After picking the chicken, Kenneth and I retired for an earnest postmortem discussion.

"Let's not tell anybody about the bill."

"O.K. Mom will never know; the head is down in the woodpile, and she won't check it out."

"No, it isn't. I threw it in the marsh."

"Do you think it hurt much?"

"No. There aren't any nerves in a chicken's beak. Haven't you seen them pecking at hard things?"

"Maybe it's like the stuff in our fingernails."

"Yeah."

"Huh! We cut her nails!"

Ned also helped lift the veil surrounding the facts of life. It might be assumed that, living so close to nature, we would have had by age eight or nine a fairly comprehensive grasp of the fundamentals. Such was not the case. We had learned only enough to generate a hundred questions. There would be no answers from my father, and as for my mother, I hardly dared think such thoughts in her presence. Though there were over a hundred cows on the plantation, their annual impregnation was a fact that simply did not exist.

Four or five big, blustery Holstein bulls were kept in pens made of concrete posts, iron pipes, and planks. The bulls were considered dangerous, and we were not to "hang around" the bull pens. Any day, quite unexpectedly, it might happen: "Now you kids go on home." There was a severe edge to my father's voice that meant, "Don't stand there gawking—get going!" We soon learned that the bull was going to be "let out." We decided to slip down to the gin house and ask Ned point-blank what this was all about. He looked at us incredulously.

"Man, how you tink we gwin a have calves on dis place if dem bulls don't mount de cows?" So that was how it was. His reply left numerous questions unanswered, but it helped. He, too, seemed reluctant to go into detail. A great many things, however, fell into place—such as roosters and dogs. That afternoon we took a circuitous route home behind a hedge of cassena bushes. They provided perfect cover—and a perfect view. Now we understood.

Ned helped only partially with another mystery. A veterinarian came several times to the barns and seemed to perform surgery on some of the mules. Our intuition told us that this was definitely not a matter to put to our father. Ned came right to the point.

"He came to castrate 'em." That answer gave us the feeling that we were supposed to know what the word meant so we said, "Why?"

"It makes 'em so we can lib wid 'em—makes 'em peaceful."

I repeated the new word several times so I wouldn't forget it before I got to a dictionary. It would be in the "c's" or "k's." The phonetic drill of those days served me well.

The horrendous act that I read in the definition left me stunned and unbelieving.

There was an occasion when Ned's presence of mind probably saved my brother's life. I learned of the terrifying experience when my parents picked us up at the close of school one afternoon early in our stay on James Island. Kenneth had not yet started school, and was in the car with them.

"What's happened to you?" my sister and I exclaimed, staring at him. There was a wide brush burn on his cheek, a cut on the edge of his scalp, and there were bandages on each hand. His big head of white hair was still touseled.

"We had a fight with Glee," he said.

"Who is Glee?"

"She's a cow that just had a calf, the only cow with a black face."
On the way home we got the full story.

The Cuthbert house, as I have said, was nearly surrounded by broad pastures where as many as seventy or eighty cows roamed. We were quite indifferent to them, playing in the pasture when we wished, or hunting for wild blackberries along the fences. A farm road, perhaps a fourth of a mile long, led from our house to the dairy buildings, the gin house, the store and the creek—a road we walked whenever we wished. Our cows showed little apprehension in open pasture, but always kept several hundred feet from a human being. One got the impression that they wanted to be left alone, and we were glad to reciprocate.

When they went to the barns that morning, my father and Kenneth were quite unprepared for what would happen. They had taken a little detour to check the windmill, and were crossing the open pasture. They were walking side by side when my father became aware that a cow had come out of the group and was striding purposefully toward them, head lowered and emitting tense, short moans, not unlike the growl of a dog. He recognized her at once as a cow named Glee, which had borne a calf several days before. The calf was put in a small pen and the mother turned out to pasture. Routine procedure—but not for Glee. At this point my father was not really disturbed, because he was experienced in the ways of cattle and confident that he knew how to handle them; he turned and shouted at her to be gone. She kept on coming, head lowered. He then drew back his heavy working shoe and delivered a kick in her nostrils—a highly sensitive area. She snorted and, head still lowered, backed away for a moment. Kenneth cried out and ran to the other side of his father. Glee gave a grunt and lunged at him. So it was this towheaded child that infuriated or attracted her. Kenneth was crying now, and my father struck out vigorously to keep his body between Kenneth and the enraged cow. By then he could see that she was not some recalcitrant or confused animal that he could deal with in the usual manner. She appeared crazed to get at this crying child.

To protect Kenneth at this juncture, he threw his arms around the animal's neck, staying behind her horns, drove his other hand into her nostrils, and prepared to throw her.

I had heard him say that a strong man can exert enough torque on a cow's neck to throw her to the ground. He wrenched with all his might and they fell to the ground together. But a frightened, angry animal doesn't stay in this position for long. He managed to hold on as she brought him again to his feet. He yelled for Kenneth to stand back, but not soon enough. With a sweep of her head she knocked him to the ground. He cried out and crawled to his feet. With my father firmly clinging to her neck, she lunged and knocked him down again. "Run for the barn!" my father shouted. "Run! Run!"

But by now the whole herd was forming into a circle of spectators. Probably the animals were not hostile, but a five-year-old boy does not easily break through a ring of horned heads. My father shouted again, "Run to the barn. Tell someone to come out here!" Kenneth started for the circle of cows, became confused, and stood motionless crying. Glee lowered her head and drove at him again. It flashed through my father's mind that a tragedy was imminent—in a twinkling his child might be trampled or gored to death. How much longer could he hold on to this mad animal?

But Ned and the omnipresent mule cart were on the way. He had been unloading some grist at the barn when he saw the circle of cows. His experience and instincts told him to act. He whipped John into a gallop, and the mule cart broke through the circle of cows. He saw a crying five-year-old boy, a charging, bellowing cow, and a man attached like a leech to her neck. He scooped Kenneth into his cart, then ran to my father's rescue. What an elderly man could do in that melee with his bare hands, I am sure he never paused to consider. He would do what he could.

My father was still clinging to Glee's neck as Ned ran up, but the cow's behavior was changing. Sensing that the cries of the child were coming from the cart, she started in that direction. My father released his hold and she pressed her nostrils against the tail of the cart, short moans coming from deep in her throat. Ned helped my father into the cart, and drove a crying, blood-spattered little boy and a gasping, disheveled man to the Cuthbert house.

When the milking was done, the boys kept Glee in the stanchion for the night. After supper my family came down to the barn to stare at her, as we might visit a zoo. Her face was indeed completely black—the only black-faced cow in the herd. When Kenneth came near her, she strained against the stanchion—swinging her head and emitting the sharp moans and grunts. What so enraged her? Did she think this child was her calf? For days the discussion went on with, of course, no answer. It was several weeks before Glee was released to the pasture, but we never trusted her. If her black face was in sight, we stayed in our yard or took a long circuitous route to the Bluff, skirting fences and hedgerows behind which we could duck if she saw us.

I never knew how Ned was selected for his position. He probably grew into it; his father had followed Wallace in his war-time migrations. No other worker on the plantation had Ned's freedom of access to supplies, feed, or toolrooms. Petty stealing was a problem on most plantations. Pieces of harness and hand tools were the items most frequently taken home after the day's work.

The offender could, of course, be referred to the constable, who would then collect a five-dollar fine at the rate of fifty cents a week. The reasoning among many planters was, "Why should the county get the money? We can impose the fine as a deterrent, and keep the money. We were the wronged party." As for Ned's stealing or being fined, it was unthinkable.

In early morning Ned rang the plantation bell that called the field hands to harness-up; he rang it again in the evening to summon them home. If a storm was threatening, he had to turn off the windmill and secure the doors and windows of the dairy barns; if a real blow was coming, he had to see that the boats were tied fast to the wharf. On a Saturday afternoon he and John and the cart might make the rounds of the plantation gates to see that all were locked—Bennetts, Thirty-six, the Farm, the Graveyard Field. He never wavered in his position of trust, and I learned years later that he died on the Bluff—still the yardman.

I never saw Ned read or write.

# 13

# *Oldest Dairy but Freshest Milk*

Mr. Lawton had spent all afternoon at the Bluff talking to my father, and as he stood on the store porch watching Mr. Lawton's old Stutz head down the creek road for Charleston, John Posey walked over from the gin house to join him. The men were silent for a moment, watching the car disappear over the little grade by the public wharf. Then Mr. Posey spoke.

"Well, what did the old man have to say this time?"

"We talked about 'the health of the plantation' as he put it. He was feeling pretty down. Wait a minute, I'm supposed to pick up a loaf of bread."

Mr. Posey was still boarding with us, and I was waiting to walk home with the men to supper. My father returned, followed by Lem Knight who locked the store and called out, "Good night, men. See you in the morning."

"It all boils down to this," my father said as we started up the path from the creek. "Our milk has to test higher in butter fat."

"Well, we always knew that. What got him started on that today?" Mr. Posey asked.

"A couple of things. Those four cows we lost last week were all high testers and that upset him. It upset all of us." My father was referring to the results of the annual tuberculin test of the herd. "Reactors"—meaning those animals that had contracted tuberculosis—had to be eliminated at once. We lost a few cows each year, much to my father's distress; his goal was to have the herd accredited—that is, free from tuberculosis.

"Then there is the marketing problem in the city. West End Dairy has just bought a new bottle of slightly different design. The neck of their new bottle is slimmer than ours is, and it makes the cream line look lower. What does the public conclude? West End Dairy's milk is richer than ours."

The value of milk then, even as now, was largely determined by its butter fat content, which varies somewhat from day to day for each cow but clusters around a mean. Every day my father tested a sample of the milk we sent to Charleston, as he did the milk that we purchased from Stiles Point plantation. The newspapers published each week the butter fat content of milk sold by the several dairies in the city; the Battery Dairy always compared favorably with its competitors.

Cecilia Lawton, whose business skill almost matched that of her late husband, was the sole owner of the Battery Dairy now that Wallace had died. Located at 41 South Battery, it had a private wharf on Murray Boulevard to which our boats from the plantation came daily. The Battery Dairy was the sole marketing agency of the milk produced on the Bluff. Cecilia had conceived of her business as serving only the "carriage trade," and her wagons, bearing the inscription "Oldest Dairy but Freshest Milk," were not allowed to deliver above Calhoun Street. Her bottling plant and wagons were neatly tucked in a lot at the foot of King Street where a condominium now stands. Most of the trade below Broad Street was hers, and certainly all of that below Tradd.

"The solution is to get some new bottles, isn't it?" asked Mr. Posey.

"Not so simple. Old Cecilia won't change. She says people can read in the papers that the Battery Dairy milk is as rich as any. But you know that for one person who reads the fine print in the paper, a hundred will see the shorter cream line on the bottle."

"I've always heard she was a stubborn old biddy," Mr. Posey said with disgust.

"Besides, the old lady likes the looks of the present bottle with the print of the two live oaks on the side; it would just cost too much to buy new ones. But they aren't helping our reputation. Someone's going to say pretty soon, 'Oldest Dairy but Bluest Milk'!"

My mother had supper ready when we arrived. We children liked to have John Posey take his meals with us because they were more varied and attractive—fewer leftovers, fewer salmon patties, and always a dessert.

My father said, as we sat around the supper table, that he had again brought up the matter of introducing new blood lines into the herd. The breeding of dairy cattle had been his special study in college, and he read continually in the professional journals on animal husbandry. Mr. Lawton acknowledged freely my father's expertise; indeed, at a state breeders' meeting in Columbia he had introduced him as "the finest dairyman in South Carolina."

"There's a good chance that I can persuade him to go along with me in bringing some new blood from a herd in Wisconsin."

I would probably not have remembered that statement if he had not followed it with, "In that case I would go to Madison myself and pick them out. Actually, I already know the ones I want but, of course, I'd have to see them."

"That would be quite a trip," John Posey observed.

"Yes, we'd buy a carload and I'd have to travel with them on the way home. I couldn't trust a load like that to the freight handlers." The talk then turned to his days at Penn State, a subject he reminisced about frequently.

While I lived on James Island I never asked myself what moti-

vated my father to leave his Pennsylvania farm and take his family to an unknown community in "the South." He must have been both "pushed" and "pulled" to make such a move. Only after many years did I sense the enormity of the decision—a man of thirty with three children under seven years of age, a product of a conservative small town and rural Pennsylvania upbringing, in no sense a drifter, sells his farm, crates up his small supply of furniture, and heads for a South Carolina plantation.

I think the "push," as I have suggested earlier, might have come from my mother's strong, omnipresent family whose members occupied land on three sides of him. There was never an open break among them, for these were people earnestly determined to live in "love and charity" with their neighbors, and rarely, I am sure, was there any openly expressed anger. But to state it simply, they annoyed him. My father was an innovative farmer; he was the first in the area to build a silo, the first to plant alfalfa, the first to align himself with the Farm Extension movement and other progressive organizations whose purpose was to improve agriculture, the first to join a dairy cooperative. In contrast, his pietistic father-in-law, after much prayer and meditation, decided to give up milk production because it required him to do business on Sunday. "Remember the Sabbath day to keep it holy . . . in it thou shalt do no manner of work; thou, and thy son, and thy daughter, thy man-servant, and thy maid-servant, thy cattle . . ."

The little farm, moreover, neat and productive though it was, did not provide my father with the opportunity to practice the principles of dairy husbandry that he had learned—and excelled in—at college. He had won national recognition as a judge of cattle at the National Dairy Show in St. Louis. He would need a larger business and much more capital than he could muster if he were to find a sense of occupational fulfillment in dairy farming.

Then, too, the traditions of his family and of his early upbringing did not prepare him for the role of a practicing farmer, though I am sure he did not sense this at the time—if he ever did. The Bresees had for many years been among the leading merchants in the county seat, a town of four thousand people. "Dye and Bresee" was the largest hardware store in the county—the only place where farmers could obtain anything from bolts and nuts to stoves, wagons, and harness; there were thousands of items in the big store on Main Street and in the four-storied warehouse behind it. The people at Dye and Bresee were proud of their benevolent, supportive position in the community; they were pleased that Saturday shoppers from the surrounding countryside would tell their children, "I'll meet you at Dye and Bresee's." The rural customers brought in vegetables, berries, and eggs, often in trade for hardware; the Bresees' relationship to them was always cordial and respectful but, I suspect, unconsciously paternalistic. After I had left James Island and was a teenager back in Pennsylvania trying to make a few dollars during the depression, I raised some fine vegetables that I hoped to sell in town. My father discouraged me in this enterprise in so many little ways that I did not take my head lettuce and sweet corn to market. He never said the words, but I sensed that the Bresees did not peddle things; they bought *from* peddlers. The old values of his childhood had surfaced without his knowing it. Probably one of the satisfactions of the managership on the Lawton plantation was that it returned my father to the entrepreneurial plateau on which he had been reared.

How did my father, town-bred, end up on a little dairy farm? As a youth he had not cared for store-clerking, a job that was being ably handled by his older brother; he was therefore permitted to spend a summer at the farm of one of the store's good customers. Soon he was spending every vacation and entire summers with this family. He was deeply happy here and spoke of the experience for the rest of his life; it was here, I have often surmised, that the resolve was born to own and operate a family farm. He was also falling in love with a girl who lived across the valley. He would finish high school, study dairy husbandry at Penn State so that he could run his farm scientifically, settle on a fertile tract of land nearby, and realize the fulfillment of his dream.

I see now that this proposed trip to Madison, Wisconsin, to select "blooded" stock for the plantation epitomized a way of life for which he had been subconsciously prepared since early childhood. His sojourn in this summit-experience would be sweet, but brief.

A trip to Wisconsin, I heard, would require at least two weeks—or more. I was disturbed at once. My father gone for two weeks?

Unthinkable. There had been times when he was quick-tempered or silent when I used to think that I didn't care if he went away for two weeks—or longer. But such a mood was short, and that was certainly not my mood now. To make matters worse, he was beginning to talk as if the trip were actually going to come off.

"You'll have to help your mother take care of things," he said one Monday evening when he was in the kitchen preparing to make one of his batches of candy. He always used to make candy on Monday nights; I never knew why.

"Are you really going to Wisconsin?"

"Yeah—looks like I'll leave this Friday afternoon. Mr. Lawton will take me over."

There was a sudden twist in my stomach, and I remember thinking, "He won't be here next Monday night to make candy, nor the next Monday . . . nor all the days in between."

"And Clyde, I think you should be responsible for taking care of the lights. You can be the only person to handle them." I felt as if my insides drained out of me and I couldn't trust myself to speak.

By "the lights" he meant the two gasoline lamps that we used each night, one in the dining room and one in the parlor. To get them to burn properly required adherence to a strict ritual. First carry them to the back porch—in case they flamed up; fill them with gasoline every other night, pump them up with a hand pump, burn two matches and heat the generator pipe while you counted to seven, open the valve slowly with the other hand until there was a soft hiss—then hope the mantle would spring to life and glow white. Much could go wrong—low gasoline supply, not enough air pressure, a broken mantle, the generator not hot enough, its aperture clogged. I had done these operations before with my father watching and enjoyed the challenge. In fact, I had often asked permission to light these lamps. Now, suddenly, I didn't want anything to do with them. I didn't want to carry them to the back porch and struggle with them—not alone!

I could see that my father was becoming quite carried away with his preparations for the trip. He also intensified his efforts to be sure that all eventualities would be cared for in his absence. I became more depressed the more he planned. I think it was on a Wednesday evening—he was to leave Friday—that we sat around the table and drew all the strands together.

"You kids can pick up the mail at the store when you come home from school," and "Kenneth, your job will be to keep the wood box full. Can you remember?"

He gave me one last lesson with the lamp on the back porch. Then he said, "I expect you to be your mother's right-hand man. You're the oldest—well, your sister's older—but you're the oldest boy. I know you'll keep your eye on things." My throat clamped so tight that I could hardly speak. I would do all these things I was supposed to do—I *knew* I would, but doing them all alone was another matter. Not alone, either, because the rest of the family would be here. Things would go on as usual, school, stopping in to talk at the Bluff, walking home to supper—wouldn't they? No, they would not! Already, I was dreading those everyday things that could never be right again. What was wrong with me? I would not say it in words, but the truth was: I could not bear the thought of his being gone. There had been times when I had imagined his being away and the thought had not disturbed me at all. But this time it was for real. Upstairs I had seen a new brown leather suitcase, and a new overcoat for the cold November days in Wisconsin. My mother had laid out his freshly ironed shirts on the spare bed. My racing imagination left me in complete turmoil. I thought I was going to cry.

My father kept on—without mercy. "I think Kenneth should be responsible for the chickens. There's enough corn in the garage to last for a week and then you can ask Ned to get you some from the gin house. Clyde, why don't you look after our milk. S. M. will fill our pail every night and you can pick it up." Here I was getting all of *his* duties and I felt worse every minute! When my father came up from the barns for supper, he carried a four-quart covered pail containing our milk for the next day. My mother started putting supper on the table when we children spotted him walking up the path from the Bluff. Now this was all over; I would walk back in the twilight alone with that pail of milk—if anyone should ever want to drink milk again.

I left the table as quietly as I could, went to my room, flung myself on the bed, buried my head in a pillow and cried. Everyone had the good sense not to follow me. The next day I did not go to school. How I ever convinced my parents that I was sick, I do not know; they were, no doubt, wiser than I thought. The rule in our house was: If you are sick enough to miss school, you stay in bed. Talking to me that day must have been so painful for all that almost no one tried. My father dropped in to say a few bright, optimistic words about all there would be for us to talk about when he got home, and how cold the weather would be up in Wisconsin. It availed nothing; the cloud of gloom about me only deepened.

Looking back from the perspective of a lifetime, I see that my father then did an incredible thing—he postponed the trip! His instincts must have told him that I needed more time to adjust to this trauma and he gave me the time. I ask now if I would have done the same thing with my children. I suspect not. I would probably have sat with them and tried to intellectualize the problem away—a futile effort, of course—and braved it through. It would have been the wrong choice.

I remember little of the days that followed his decision to wait, except that slowly my anxiety subsided. We talked freely about the trip, about trains, we studied maps, and the future began to look bright again. Toward the end of the week my father left, and I did not cry.

# 14

# *Jamsie*

Anyone with time on his hands eventually drifted down to the wharf; the store was there if you had an extra penny or a nickel, and there were always the boats. The wharf attracted all the boys on the plantation. The *Palmetto* and the *Virginia,* carrying milk twice daily to Charleston and returning with freight, were either coming or going. They were typical low-country freight boats, thirty to forty feet long, shallow-hulled to negotiate the tidal creeks. Bench seats for passengers were built around the stern and up each side. A cabin covered the rear half of the "hold," and in bad weather canvas could be stretched over the front half. These launches, as Mr. Lawton called them, were powered by a one- or two-cylinder make-and-break engine placed low in the boat behind an exposed, oversized flywheel. These awkward-looking engines did not whir and hum as modern ones do; they started with a series of jerky explosions that finally settled down into a steady put-put-put. There was no other sound quite like this in the low country, and our boats announced their coming around the bend of the creek long before they were visible.

They provided the most convenient and direct route to downtown Charleston. To reach the Battery Dairy by car meant an eight-mile journey over sand roads, crossing the Ashley two miles upstream, and then traveling down to the end of the peninsula. James Island Creek provided the Bluff an outlet to the harbor and city at either high or low tide. As the stream wound back through the marshland to other plantations, it offered them access only at high tide. Workers on the Bluff might ride to Charleston on the *Palmetto* or the *Virginia* by paying the regular fare of fifteen cents a trip. There were few perquisites on the Bluff for the Negro hands. In the city it was otherwise.

The creek that flowed by the Lawton plantation is linked in my memory with Jamsie. It was on its banks, and at the wharf that jutted out from the plantation store, that my brother and I most often met him. As we had now so thoroughly learned, he could not properly play at our house or swing on the big rope that hung from one of the oaks in our yard. Kenneth and I could not play at his house by the bend in the creek. It would not have looked quite right. So it was at the water's edge, or at the marshy inlet behind our house, that we could play and cause offense to no one.

Jamsie was a little taller, a little stronger, and he knew every-thing. "Yeah, man, I can fix dat." He fairly radiated confidence and know-how about boats and the marshlands. Fishing out at the bend of the creek in the afternoon, we would see thunderheads looming darkly to the northwest. "Man, I tink we bettah wind up dese lines and pull dat anchor." And so we did. After tying up at the wharf, we would wade up the mud bank with our croakers, whiting, and catfish. Jamsie would dress the catfish for his mother. White folks never ate catfish.

Jamsie's father had disappeared years ago, died or moved away, and I don't think Jamsie ever knew him. His mother, Josephine, lived in a little house beyond the public wharf and kept herself alive doing field work and taking in washings. She was a small, vigorous woman who laughed a lot, and had a cheerful way of waving her apron when you left. Of course, we never played around her door or even in her area. Josephine bore a heavy bur-den—it was her oldest son, Crazy John. To me, as a child, he was not a burden; he was a curiosity, with just enough danger about him to be exciting. He wandered all day up and down the creek, all the while shouting unintelligible things at us. He wore a tattered burlap sack from his shoulders that rarely covered him decently, and to our fascinated eyes, he was obviously not a little boy. He couldn't talk, we were told, and he slept out of doors at night.

While Jamsie fished with us on the wharf, we would see John wandering over the mud banks half a mile away searching for crabs. When he found one, he would crush it in his hands and eat it raw. He was probably a victim of syphilis or epilepsy. I am sure there was never a diagnosis. Who could pay for a diagnosis, and what would his mother do with it if she had one? In those days "Crazy John" was Josephine's problem, and hers alone.

I never knew that Jamsie ever went to school. He was evasive to our questioning. On James Island in those days the Negro children rarely went beyond "foth book," and many not that far.

He worked on neighboring plantations when truck crops were gathered and during cucumber picking helped us on the Bluff. My brother and I were allowed to break caste long enough to help in the cucumber harvest. There was almost no productive work that a white boy could do on a plantation, but when the fifteen-acre field of cucumbers was ready for picking and every available hand was needed, Kenneth and I were allowed to join the throng of women and children that streamed over the field. The pay was four cents a bushel. Mule carts were stationed at strategic points on the field roads into which we could empty our burlap bags and baskets, and get credit from the field foreman. Jamsie often worked in rows adjacent to ours rather than beside his mother, Josephine. If we indulged in too much horse play—like throwing cull cucumbers at each other—the field foreman would call to us to quiet down. When Kenneth's bag of cucumbers grew heavy—

Kenneth was the smallest of us three—Jamsie would jump over into his row and pull it forward for him. We loved the days of cucumber picking. They came just as school was out in the spring, and seemed more like a festival than hard work. It was the only time when Jamsie and I could earn money side by side.

The day we decided to roast English sparrows, Jamsie was playing with us in that big, three-storied resource center down by James Island Creek—the gin house. One of our favorite diversions was to drop in and surprise a hundred English sparrows feeding on a pile of ground corn in one of the upper rooms. Once a week the men started the big engine on the first floor to grind corn for the mules and cattle, storing it in a high-ceilinged room with large glass windows on two sides. We liked to creep softly up the stairs and suddenly pop the door open on a flock of sparrows. They would fly to the windows in a whirring, chirping cloud, crash into the glass, and fall back, partially stunned.

Watching these plump birds gorging on cornmeal may have given us the idea. It was an easy one to come by, because we killed and ate a variety of birds on the Bluff. There were geese and chickens, as a matter of course, and my father brought home partridges, doves, rice birds, and marsh hens, all of which we helped him dress on the back porch. I think it was Jamsie who said it first. "Let's get some of those birds and build a fire and roast 'em. Dey is almost as big as rice birds." Making a little fire was a fascination none of us could resist. We were perfectly sure that if we asked for a few matches and permission to build a fire, the answer would be no. Our fires therefore were always made secretly, in the little nooks and by-ways down at the Tide. Jamsie usually had matches. Capture some game? Have a feast? The day was shaping up!

Back to the storage room in the gin house. The sparrows rose in a cloud as usual, and we soon had collected half a dozen stunned birds. Luckily, Jamsie had a knife, sparing us the awkwardness of borrowing my mother's kitchen knife. We had seen the men skin partridges, and knew exactly how to go about it. Then to the mule trough where there was a faucet of running water; we soon had half a dozen birds ready for the fire and were heading across the pasture for the Tide. Jamsie had picked up a short piece of wire at the gin house. "We'll put 'em on dis wire to roast 'em," he said. My brother and I found no fault with this idea.

There were a dozen hidden paths and open spots in the thicket of cassena that bordered the Tide. We found one that we thought was well concealed and scooped out a pit in the ground with a trench leading in the direction of the wind. From here on everyone helped—hunting bits of firewood, setting up little Y-shaped sticks to hold the spit, and poking the fire.

How long does one turn a sparrow over a smoky fire? No one knew, and if we had wanted to time it, no one had a watch. A pleasant odor began to mingle with the wood smoke. The little forms on the wire—dark to begin with—were getting almost black now. Jamsie poked one with the point of his knife. To our surprise, the heat had made it hard, not tender. Though no one would admit it, those hard little pieces of meat began to look less and less appetizing. No doubt we had been hurrying the process a bit; we began to think our birds would never be tender. Someone opined that we should have cooked them in a pot, the way you do chicken. We pushed one off the wire and tried to cut it. Some dark, stringy breast meat broke off. Finally, I volunteered to take a taste. "It's not done yet," I said. "It tastes a little like chicken."

"I don't think it will taste very good without salt," my brother said. He, at least, had an excuse for not eating English sparrow. No one was willing to go in search of salt. We were still having fun—the seclusion of our little retreat and the fire in the pit. But no one talked about eating.

"I tink we ought to roast 'em a little longer," Jamsie said as he got up and surveyed the fire.

The little birds smoked and sizzled, but they were slowly becoming unrecognizable lumps.

"Let's go check the tide," my brother said. "I feel like doing something." We walked over to the little stream of water that was backing in from the Ashley River. "Looks like the tide is half in."

"Yeah, it's getting late," I said. "It must be about five o'clock." A person who watches the tides closely can tell the time of day to within a half hour. The other boys agreed that it was getting late—very late. Did each of us now have an excuse for not eating roasted English sparrow?

We returned to the fire. "Let's push some dirt over it and go home," someone said. "And we can throw the birds back in the bushes for a possum."

"Dat possum better have good teeth," Jamsie said. We headed for our house and Jamsie took the path across the pasture to Josephine's house.

That night at the supper table my brother suddenly said, "Clyde shouldn't be hungry tonight. This afternoon he filled up on roasted sparrow." I had been afraid of this all day—Kenneth's love of entertaining.

"What *are* you talking about?" my mother exclaimed.

To answer that question took the next few minutes of fast, loud talking. "I only tasted one. A sparrow isn't any dirtier than a chicken or a partridge. I was just curious."

My older sister looked up from her plate and said, "I can't believe my ears!"

My mother uttered her usual exclamation of dismay, "Well, for conscience sake!"

My father almost never laughed out loud, but that night I heard him chuckle.

While the ebbing tide in James Island Creek was swift and almost mean, the ebb tide in the inlet behind our house was swift but safe. The tiny stream that wandered through this low ground would carry our little boats and rafts into Charleston harbor if we did not anchor them with string. The basic channel, if it could be called that, seemed to emerge from a V-shaped indentation of marsh land bordering the Ashley River. As the little stream entered the basin behind our house, it flowed past banks of cassena bushes and around the gnarled rots of water oaks. We could sit on the exposed roots of one old tree and try to catch blue crabs that had been left by the receding tide.

Jamsie often joined us here. Josephine imposed few restrictions on his movements, and he could wander the plantation freely to discover excitement. We always wanted Jamsie to play at the Tide, but our meetings were coincidental—or seemed so. There was no telephone, and if there had been, neither of us could have called the other. It was unthinkable that either of us could approach the other's mother with a request for someone to come outside and play. By watching the tides and our comings and goings, Jamsie could meet us often at the little inlet behind our house.

One morning in early summer we were down at the Tide in a high state of excitement. At the movies the night before we had seen a tragically beautiful spectacle—a ship had put out to sea with its sails on fire! Under much pressure, my mother had taken my brother and me to see a movie called *The Vikings*, at the Academy of Music in Charleston. We left the theater with a consuming desire to make a boat and set it adrift in the Tide with the sails on fire. We had been playing in the water only a few minutes that morning when we saw Jamsie coming across the pasture.

Jamsie had never seen a movie. The words theater, motion picture, screen meant nothing to him. What he may have concluded about the Vikings from our excited descriptions, we did not wait to discover. We plunged ahead with our plans and he caught our enthusiasm at once. He saw immediately the possibilities of a spectacle—and a lot of fun.

Making a boat presented problems. We could get a little wooden box from the plantation store and caulk the cracks, as we had seen people along James Island Creek do almost every day. But to produce a craft that wouldn't leak would take time—several days, possibly. We were impatient to get on with the burning. There must be a better solution.

Something substantial, something wooden, something that would float. I don't know whether Kenneth or I said the words first—"Mother's chopping bowl!" It was oval-shaped, about eighteen inches long and six inches deep, and hewn from a single block of wood. She used it to chop cabbage for cole slaw. It wouldn't sink and was ready for immediate service. Would our mother part with the bowl? I realize now, wonderingly and a little proudly, that we never considered "snitching" it or "borrowing" it as viable possibilities. We felt she would yield to the proper frontal attack.

Jamsie waited at the Tide while Kenneth and I raced for the kitchen door. Surely my mother would understand the rich possibilities in the chopping bowl as a sail boat! I know now that she had no books on child development, and the term "creative play" was not in her vocabulary. But she had imagination. She had many times allowed us to remove the belt from her treadle sewing machine, place our own string belt around the flywheel and then, operating the treadle with our hands, produce a power source that would drive our Erector Set creations at enormous speeds. Our arguments for the Viking craft must have been convincing, because we soon left with the chopping bowl and her parting admonition, "Don't let it float away into Charleston harbor!"

Then off to the shop in the gin house where there were nails, pieces of wood, and wire. Jamsie came to the fore here; his ignorance of Viking culture was of no consequence. Using many guy wires, he helped us set up a firm mast without punching a hole in the bottom of the bowl. He must have found a piece of white cloth somewhere because we finally had a big square sail attached to the mast, with the whole affair held erect by wires and strings that reached down to the "deck" of the chopping bowl. We admired it for half an hour and were tempted to try it out in James Island Creek, but the possibility that it might drift away from us was so real that we decided to use it only at the Tide. Here the little stream, perhaps four feet wide, that wound its way through low ground would permit us to walk beside our vessel as the wind and tide carried it along.

I think it was Jamsie who thought we ought to put something like kerosene or turpentine on the sail to make it burn. The cloth would just smoke, he thought. We chose turpentine because it somehow did not sound as dangerous as kerosene.

We headed across the pasture for the Tide, bearing our contraption between us as if it were the Ark of the Covenant. The Ashley River and the moon had obliged us beautifully that afternoon. A big tide had filled the winding stream of our inlet to its banks, and the water was only now returning to the sea.

"Jamsie, you can set it on fire."

"No, man. You boys do dat." He took the mooring line, tugging at the craft gently as it rocked in the wind. "We sure do a good job on dat mast and sail. It don't tip at all."

We were all holding back on lighting the match. My brother

and I might have quarreled over who should do it if Jamsie had not been there. A quarrel would have destroyed Jamsie's big smile and easy grace—something, we sensed, wordlessly, that must not be allowed to happen. We did not know anything then about the subject of human relations; we knew only that when Jamsie played with us we laughed a lot and never quarreled. Half a lifetime later I would sense how rare his gentle spirit was. He finally took the matches we pressed into his hands, and kneeling on the bank, put the fire to the sail. The turpentine-soaked cloth only smoldered.

"We need more heat," Jamsie called out. "You all got to help me."

My brother and I began striking matches. Suddenly the sail ignited.

"Man, oh, man, look at dat," Jamsie exclaimed. We pushed our little craft into the main stream and let the tide and breeze take over.

With a short pole we guided our doomed ship around one bend and then another. The ebbing tide was carrying us steadily toward the harbor and the sail was burning briskly. We ducked under overhanging cassena bushes and around the heavy roots of oak trees. Then the shore became muddy underfoot. Our little stream was opening into a wider stretch of marsh grass where it would soon lose its identity. We were leaving the little basin called the Tide, and it was time to bring our Viking craft to shore. The sails were a smoky ruins. Some little strips of wood were burning in the bottom of the bowl in a most gratifying manner. We doused the smoldering sails, half filling the bowl with water. It had been a good enterprise, one that had worked even better than we had dreamed. We also knew, intuitively, that the voyage could not be repeated; we must dismantle the ship and head for home with the chopping bowl.

Returning the bowl to its original condition was not the simple task that we had envisioned. There were scorch marks, and an offensive odor of turpentine. We paused a moment to consider the problem and to plan a story for our mother. But Jamsie, the facilitator, was there.

"Let's get some sand and scrub dis ting. I see my mother do dat sometimes."

We scrubbed until our fingers were sore and most of the black was removed; we still eyed with concern the few remaining brown stains. My mother, as it turned out, said almost nothing about them. I think she accepted the triumphant account of our venture that afternoon as full compensation for any damage to her chopping bowl.

As we left the inlet, we came to the path that led across the pasture to Jamsie's house. We paused to say goodbye. A walk up to our back porch would only be awkward. Each of us knew that our day must end here at the edge of the Tide. Until we met tomorrow, Jamsie would return to his world and we to ours. Moreover, Kenneth and I were getting hungry for a peanut butter sandwich.

As I approached adolescence, Jamsie and I saw a little less of each other. For me, there were books and music lessons, more trips to Charleston, a succession of hobbies—chemistry sets, insect collecting, stamps—which came and went almost with the seasons. Jamsie could not join me here. The *Youth's Companion* and Horatio Alger books began to steal time from the creek, and mothers on James Island were beginning to plan little parties where we could learn ballroom dancing. I would soon be going to the High School of Charleston. I cannot remember any change in my feeling for Jamsie, but I sensed that he was changing, at least in outward behavior and, I suppose, he thought the same of me. When we met, his face always lighted up in a full-faced grin, but there was less to talk about. I knew he was wondering how long he could meet me on a first-name basis. When should it be "Mistuh Clyde?" Once I thought I heard a "sir" slip into his talk, but I am not sure.

In time I went to high school, Jamsie got work in Charleston, and I never saw him again. My repeated inquiries on returning to James Island years later produced the same responses. "I tink he gone to Savannah. He nevah come back to dis island." "Duh cities done swallow Jamsie up."

After I had moved away from James Island, and as hard times intensified in the thirties, I kept track of my white friends. We could, and did, write to each other. One had to drop out of college, another went to a CCC camp, another worked in a store. Why did I not wonder how Jamsie was getting on? Would I never eradicate the double standard? Jamsie would be happy with less. He didn't really have to get on. He would find his place somehow and "make do." He always had. Not everyone is supposed to do "big things." If you don't expect big things, you aren't disappointed. Josephine and Crazy John had not worried me very much. Why should Jamsie?

I wish now that the day we sailed our Viking chopping bowl I had brought Jamsie a peanut butter sandwich, and that we could have eaten together before he went home that night. But I didn't. A fine, invisible wire wound its serpentine way through all our relationships. I stopped, unthinking, whenever I bumped into it. I never tested its strength.

Jamsie, true friend of my boyhood, if the big cities did not do you in, if, uneducated and unskilled, you were not overwhelmed by the flotsam and jetsam of life, I should like to greet you again and say, "I loved you, but I was too blind or mindless to know it."

# 15

# *Riding the Crops*

It was twelve o'clock noon on the Fourth of July. The double doors of the club house stood open, people were lounging in chairs on the two broad porches, and the school ground was filling with cars. The little club house—more correctly, the Agricultural Hall—was opening its arms to the planters and their families for the social and gastronomic event of the year—the annual picnic meeting of the James Island Agricultural Society.

There was much for the ladies to do. The floor of the little stage had to be disassembled and turned into long dining tables which, in turn, were to be mounted on sawhorses. Rows of plates and silver were set out, and the children carried chairs. No one knew for certain when the dinner would begin. It would depend upon when the men rode in on their horses.

For the planters, the Fourth of July had begun early; before they could settle down for their afternoon dinner at the hall, they would have "ridden the crops." At our place Ned would saddle up Prince, my father's horse, early in the morning while the air was yet cool and tie him outside our door ready for my father to ride. For this occasion he wore khaki-colored pants, a blue shirt with a stiff collar, a tie, and a hat—the standard attire of planters. I watched him as he cantered off to Stiles Point plantation to join a dozen other men for their annual inspection of the crops in midsummer.

The cucumbers, potatoes, and green beans had been harvested, and corn, velvet beans, sorghum, and a few fields of cotton were in full swing. After making the rounds of the plantations the group would head for the James Island School ground, hungry and ready for the traditional dinner. Membership in the historic James Island Agricultural Society was restricted to planters on James Island; my father could be a member by virtue of his position as plantation manager. If the Society undertook scientific or educational activities, I was not aware of them; the annual meeting on the Fourth was the event of the year. It always culminated in a lavish picnic dinner at the club house, to which wives, children, and a few Charleston bankers were invited.

As the men rode, they shared their experiences with seeds, fertilizers, and labor problems. An informal consensus was reached as to the planter who had the best field of cotton or velvet beans. The planters were not in competition with each other; there were no trade secrets. A fine cotton crop on Stono could not diminish the one at Sea Side. They sought to learn from each other.

Though there were still large plantings of truck crops and some cotton on the island, several of the planters were now adding small dairy herds. The sale of milk could provide a steady cash flow in contrast to the seasonal and highly variable earnings from such crops as potatoes, cucumbers, and beans. The addition of small dairies meant that the concerns of these planters were moving more closely to those of my father and Mr. Lawton. Since a cow's milk production is directly related to intake of protein, increasing attention was paid to the raising of such high-protein foods as corn, sweet potatoes, and velvet bean hay. The fact that the Bluff was willing to purchase milk wholesale from neighboring plantations probably spurred the trend toward dairying. At one time or another the Bluff bought milk from Stono, Stiles Point, Seaside, and Centerville.

While the uncertain New York vegetable price quotations were the chief source of anxiety for the more traditional planters, the gnawing problem at the Bluff was a disease—bovine tuberculosis. The complete eradication of the disease would mean that the herd could be officially accredited, a goal that my father thought supremely important. Try as he might to conquer the disease by eliminating any animal that was "positive" in the annual test, new cases appeared and the loss of cows to the city abattoir continued.

My father then decided upon a drastic course of action that was based on two hypotheses—the testing was not done often enough, and the test was not discriminating enough. Sick cows were getting by. While his fellow, neophyte dairymen admired his courage for initiating semiannual testing, they could not be persuaded to adopt the plan for their own herds. The success of the second hypothesis would depend on his own diagnostic skill—a combination of intuition and scientific observation. He asked the state health authorities to pay the indemnity for the cows he selected—although the state had already declared them to be well— if they proved upon examination to have the disease. Should they turn out to be healthy, the plantation would take the loss. The state agreed to cooperate in this novel tactic. At the next testing my father added eight cows to the condemned list. The abattoir veterinarians found that all eight were suffering from tuberculosis, two so seriously that they had to be "tanked," the vernacular for totally destroyed.

In addition to discussing the income-producing activities of the plantations; the Agricultural Society had to consider the matter of labor. If there was any competition among the planters, it was in the matter of securing "hands," as the field workers were called. Even here, a firm but unwritten gentlemen's code prevailed; there was nothing among the planters that approached pirating of labor. Each plantation had its core of black families that never moved about; these steady workers were the ideal employees and strong emotional ties often developed between them and their employers. There were also transients, many of whom were good workers, but they were restless. They might be men who had come from the city when work was slack, or older youths who wanted a different life, or cousins from upstate. At certain seasons every plantation needed extra help, yet no planter actually sought to lure workers from his neighbors. Somehow the "code" worked, although certain plantations were regarded as better places to work than others. Housing, agreeable foremen, and perquisites like wood and garden land varied among the plantations.

There was, however, another consideration affecting workers on James Island that could be traced directly to the annual meeting of the James Island Agricultural Society—the setting of the pay rate for the ensuing year. I remember hearing numbers like eight and ten cents an hour being discussed. This was the rate for plowing, chopping cotton, and other routine field work. Would the members of the Society stand as one on this matter? On the Bluff, where there was a large herd of cows, the boys in the dairy could earn more, and no one would question it. Their work was more demanding; to me they were more alert and more interesting than the field men. Planters could reserve the right to set their own rewards for specialized workers, following the practice of slavery days; house boys, yardmen, and groomsmen received favored treatment, and earned the envy, if not the love, of the field hands. At any rate, the Society reached a firm consensus—informally, of course—on the matter of hourly pay.

Following the big dinner I sat on the club house porch listening to the men talk. The teenagers had taken off for Folly Beach and there weren't enough younger ones left for games. It was easy to drift over to the edge of the porch, kick little trenches in the sand

with my toes, and listen. Among the men lounging on the porch
that afternoon there must have been a dozen who had been boys
or young men when the Civil War ended; in a haze of cigar smoke
they sat and reminisced from direct experience.

In the late 1860s, they agreed, James Island had been in a state
of economic collapse; only six plantation houses had survived the
occupation. The white families, most of whom had fled further
inland, returned to James Island to salvage their plantations, rebuild their houses, and form some kind of local government. Former slaves, organized and led by adventurers from the North,
were a constant menace.

"We had to do something to show them who had the authority
around here," I heard one man say. "So we formed ourselves into
a sort of drill team—a kind of militia. This didn't break any laws
and it sent the message we wanted. And we used to drill right over
there, every Saturday afternoon," he said, pointing to the open
space in front of the school. "This was no secret meeting," he went
on, "we let everybody know what we were up to. We were called
the Haskell Mounted Riflemen. It was a kind of preventive measure. The men drilled and we did a little target practice. We made
sure the Negroes came to watch. We kept this up for several years;
it did a lot to restore law and order." He stopped and thoughtfully
shook his head. "This was a busy place on Saturdays."

By late afternoon the Society had elected its officers for the
coming year, and the women had carried their picnic baskets to
the cars. The meeting had broken up into little groups. With
much handshaking and tipping of hats, the men moved toward
their horses.

We left the empty school ground to the mockingbirds and stray
dogs. Coming back to the school in midsummer always made me
feel lonesome, and today was no exception. The grass had grown
tall where we played in the spring, but the great pines sighed and

the windmill creaked. As we drove away the sun was low, and the trees cast long shadows across the playground. Or was it a parade ground . . . where grim, erect men rode back and forth flourishing their weapons, and black faces peered from the hedgerows?

## *16*

# *No Harmful Influence*

From his plantation on James Island, St. John Alison Lawton had written to my father before we left Pennsylvania: "In looking over your letters, I noticed what you said about the negro question. I think you might have some trouble in managing negro labor, but I think there would be no harmful influence on your children. The negroes are not our intimates."

My father had raised the racial issue after his first visit to James Island. I do not know what he feared. Probably his greatest fear was for the unknown. In a week's visit he could not have discovered the elaborate complex of tradition, manners, and bedrock convictions that governed the relations between the black and white races in those days.

"The negroes are not our intimates." Alison Lawton was right, so long as he did not mean to imply that this deep-rooted subculture would have no influence upon us. For it did. The cultures were not that distinct. The social strictures imposed by the white people could not obscure the essential humanity that I kept discovering daily on the plantation. Alison Lawton's people and mine may have had a monopoly on property and what goes with it; they had no monopoly on tenderness, or humor, or religious devotion, or love of family.

In this strange new world of blacks and whites working together on a plantation, would there be some insidious influence of which my father was not aware? Perhaps it was the disquieting thought that his children might "fall into bad company" that concerned him. The Negroes had strange ways, a strange way of talking, and certainly inferior living conditions. He knew that his family would observe poverty as they had never seen it before. Life within the little shacks was stripped of nearly all the protections of privacy that he had known in the North. The basic life functions were plain for all to see. Courtship, procreation, death, the struggle for food and clothing found few places to hide in a two-room cabin.

His children would, in a disturbing sense, "grow up" sooner here; perhaps that was what my father feared. Certainly there was "no harmful influence" in the sense that the Negroes promoted in us lying, or cheating, or disobedience, or sexual immorality. Surely they did not tempt us to drink or gamble. Neither did they present the subtle temptation that parents fear for their children—the temptation to accept low goals. For as much as I came to like and to depend upon my Negro friends, they did not, and could not, ever have served as vocational models for me.

What my father could not know, in those days of decision, was that in the midst of poverty and ignorance I would also see whole families struggling heroically to maintain dignity against powerful forces that would degrade them. As for his fears? He might much more justifiably have feared that his eldest son would become "rank conscious"—which he did—and what is worse, that he would be quite unaware of this change in his personality. Though I did not know it was happening at the time, almost at once I became a part of the dual "we" and "they" culture.

Alison Lawton knew, of course, that with rank and privilege goes responsibility, and in one of his letters he offered this insight:

As fine and honest and refined people have grown up on these Sea Islands, as you will find anywhere in the country. The negroes have been

taught to look up to the white people. This requires strict honesty on
the part of the white people, and a negro would trust a white man rather
than one of their own race. They are respectful of white people. On the
whole seacoast of South Carolina there has never been known an at-
tempted case of rape; and there never have been lynchings or that kind
of carrying on as there has been in some parts of the South.

One would like to think that living among so many people who
were losers on almost every count would have developed my sense
of compassion and sympathy. At the time, I regret to say, it did
not. I quickly learned that the "theys" had different needs and
values. Do not try to change this fact. Do not try to understand
"them" by extrapolating the "we" values. "They" are different, and
let that fact remain. Whether this moral blind spot of my childhood was ultimately harmful to me I shall never know. I like to
think that when the perceptual shift in me did occur, I had been
sensitized by the James Island experience, and made more loving
than I might otherwise have been. I have no solid evidence to
support this hope.

Sexuality on the plantation met my eyes at every turn. The
weather was hot and clothing was scarce and ill-fitting. I saw the
human body spilling out of dresses that were too small, and pro-
truding from clothing with missing buttons. If my parents had
nothing to say about the relations of men and women and the
origins of life, I learned it in outbursts from the dairy boys. I was
absorbed by their easy banter, laughter, and pantomime as they
relived the events of the night before. Their talk helped to clear
up the mystery of the James Island roads after dark. Those saun-
tering couples who disappeared in the hedgerows as our headlights approached had always set my fantasy going; now it had
something to work on. Whatever I couldn't imagine, Oscar would

tell me in exquisite detail as he milked the cows. There were clearly some delicious experiences that these big guys had which I knew nothing about. These boys weren't fooling—it was good! I could learn the most from them if I pretended to know what they were talking about. I wasn't stupid enough to try to make them think that I had sneaked off into the bushes with anyone; I just pretended that I knew "how things were"—they wouldn't have to talk down to me. I soon learned the names of girls on the plantation who had something to offer. I now watched Victoria with fresh interest when she came barefoot into the store to buy for her mother. Her breasts played hide-and-seek behind a tattered dress that hung loosely from her shoulder. I also watched her hips. Oscar said, "She sure know how to use 'em—just like when she walk."

Sex was thickest in the store on Friday night after the payoff. I stayed behind the counter where I was allowed to sell penny candy. I would reach into a glass case while the men pointed out their selections. "I want tree cent wut of merry jane, two silber bell, and one jaw-bone broker." I put the candy in a little bag and took the nickel.

In early evening, people would drift in from neighboring plantations, packing the little store full of men and girls out for a night of socializing. Bodies touched and hands were busy. What else could you do on Friday night if you had no transportation and no money? It cost nothing to take a short walk over to the Bluff Store where you could find new people to mess around with, share a bottle of Try-Me, maybe seduce someone—or be seduced. The theme of the night was bodies. What else? No radio, no telephone, no newspapers. No one had read anything. Make the most of what you have—people.

I liked them and these people liked me. I understood every nuance of their Gullah talk and I was beginning to understand their body talk—this uninhibited pleasure that grown-ups took in closeness. They knew I was the manager's boy, and they treated me that way. I was a spectator—never a participant—an observer of something I barely understood. I would always see Oscar and Eddie, and other dairy boys there on these Friday nights. One night Oscar sat on the cover of the oat bin, laughing as always. Victoria came over and backed up between his legs and settled herself against his body. He held her with his hands cupped around her breasts. He snuggled his face against her neck; they were in great good humor. Then he caught my eye and winked. I winked back. Comrades we were—this tall, rangy boy smiling at me and enveloping his girl with his long arms. We understood—didn't we?—what only men can know—the secret delights of maleness. Didn't we? It was as if a door to another room had been suddenly pushed ajar. What I saw attracted me—and frightened me, but I knew that someday I would push the door open and enter.

A great beauty came to us soon after we arrived on James Island; it came at the time Samuel Brown died—straight from the heart of the black culture. Sam, a foreman and the most respected man on the Bluff, died in his cabin by the dairy barns at the age of seventy-five. He had belonged to two burial societies, "The Sons and Daughters of I Shall Rise" and "The Sons and Daughters of Jerusalem." A faithful dues payer all his life, he was now to reap the benefits of his sacrifice. Jointly, these societies would put on his funeral; a better wording might be: jointly they would produce the pageant that was his funeral. On the day before he was to be buried, boatloads of Negroes from the city docked at the public wharf on our place. They came with fine clothing, trumpets, banners, and drums. Burial was to be in a cemetery on the eastern edge of the plantation. Two parts of this impressive event stand out in my memory: the procession to the grave and the "setting up" of the evening before. The procession, even though it was over a mile long—reaching from the dairy barns to the cucumber field—turned out to be only a colorful parade; but the singing prayer meeting of the night before the burial was a spiritual experience.

At the edge of the Negro section and across the pasture from the Cuthbert house was a rectangular assembly hall that might hold a hundred people. It was here that the faithful gathered, overflowing into the surrounding field. By air line, the hall was about a quarter of a mile from our home. The singing began just after dusk. The first chorus had brought us onto the front porch. We tiptoed back into the house for chairs, as if afraid to break a spell, and sat there in the dark. There was no radio playing next door, and no whine of tires on a highway. Neither were there any street lights to spoil the soft outlines of the night. The sea breeze that came in daily over the low land gently stirred the leaves in our live oaks. Except for the whisper of the trees, there was silence. Like a hushed, expectant audience in a great theater, we waited for the next song.

A woman's high voice led off in a plaintive falling cadence: "An-y-how, an-y-how . . ." Then the congregation joined in a rising swell—

> An-y-how, my Lawd.
> At duh cross whe 'E die,
> I'm gwina go to he-ben, any-how.

Stanza after stanza floated over the fields.

> You can 'cuse me,
> You can 'buke me,
> I'm gwina go to heben—anyhow.

They moved to clapping and shouting songs: "Eb'ry one who is libin got to die" . . . "Down in duh wally, on my prayin knees" . . . "Gwine to res' from all my labuh, Lawd."

This was more than singing. This was a deep comradeship that carried them up and beyond their daily round. This was the music of brotherhood and hope and the brooding presence of God. I had never heard men and women sing as if they had lost all awareness of the world about them. Their soaring voices told of a fellowship that we sitting on the front porch could not join. I had no words for what I felt then, but in the music that drifted across the fields that night another door for me was gently pushed ajar— a door that opened upon a new and mystical world. I was filled with a longing that I had never known before.

# 17

# *Martha Love Rivers*

Martha Love Rivers was our link between yesterday and tomorrow. If she had a little stronger grip on yesterday than most, it was not hard to understand why. The war had destroyed much of the wealth of her ancestors, and the lives of many of them. While the battle of Secessionville, fought on the Rivers's plantation, had been a rout for the enemy, it had left only two buildings standing.

Though she was a conservator of the past, she was not gloomy about it; the world she taught us was a bright, fascinating place, and the only way to have any fun was to get busy and find out all you could about it. She was the only person I knew who had been to the Grand Canyon, stood under the giant sequoias, seen a volcano, walked on a glacier. Here was the evidence to prove it, pictures, a piece of petrified wood, a hunk of lava. Parents probably said that geography and history were her strong points; we of the fifth and sixth grades thought she was good in everything.

If the wrongs her family had suffered in the past embittered her, we never sensed it. Naturally, we learned that great injustices had been done to earnest, loyal Americans. "States' rights" had been violated, trampled on by superior forces; just causes, we must remember, did not always win—that was one of the mysteries of life—but the heroism and devotion of the Confederates left them really victors, if not on the field of battle, surely on the fields of history.

To be sure, there were certain principles that a daughter of a

Confederate captain practiced as a matter of course. One never mentioned Abraham Lincoln's name; no harangues against him— he simply did not exist. You do not talk about a non-person or, as a matter of fact, about anything he has written. It all seemed natural enough to me. Our history book said substantially the same thing. It was my parents who discovered that we had not read two selections in our reading book: the Gettysburg Address and Lincoln's letter to Mrs. Bixby.

"Did you like this?" one of my parents said, pointing to the Gettysburg Address.

"We didn't read it," I said.

"What? How come?"

"Oh, I don't know. Miss Rivers said we would skip it." For me there could be no better reason.

My parents did more turning of pages. Apparently an idea was beginning to dawn.

"How about this?" pointing to the famous letter.

"We didn't read that, either."

"Well, I declare!"

My folks liked Miss Rivers and admired her greatly, and whatever they might have thought about her choice of reading selections, they were not about to put her down in front of us.

In the sixth grade we used an abridged edition of William Gilmore Simms's *History of South Carolina,* first published in 1840 and thereafter revised to encompass subsequent developments. I remember little of the "history" it may have contained; I do remember the aura of nobility and heroism that enveloped all the men in the book. Miss Rivers taught William Gilmore Simms faithfully. The Revolutionary War was won, as I remember, by the Swamp Fox (he operated a few miles from James Island), and the Battle of King's Mountain. As for "The War Between the States," it was the sterling character of the Confederate soldiers that we must remember; they fought against well-equipped, overfed, overpaid soldiers who fought only for money, and who really didn't win in the deep sense—there were just so many of them. I never learned until many years later that Charleston had been occupied and James Island overrun by the enemy. There were certain things one didn't talk about in the presence of children.

When I entered the High School of Charleston several years later, one of my teachers said to several of us James Islanders, "Are they still using that Simms's history over there?"

At once I felt defensive; this was another crack at the "country kids." I wanted to say, "Yeah, what of it?" but one did not say that to a teacher. I said, "Yes, sir."

"God! That's the most biased book I ever read!"

I reeled at such blasphemy.

The "school library," all donated, offered Miss Rivers and her twenty-five pupils the use of parts of two sets of books, *The Boy Allies and the Great War* and an adventure series for girls called the *Ruth Fielding* books. We went through these in short order. All the rest, besides the textbooks, she had to bring—from somewhere. When her Model-T coupé came to a stop behind the school each morning, there was a group of children waiting to carry in the things she had collected the night before—much of it, I suspect, bought with her own money. Sheets of cardboard, *National Geographic* magazines, cloth, crayons, nails, water colors, a mortar and pestle. There was no limit. One day a portable phonograph appeared, a small, wind-up affair that she would use to play Walter Camp's physical exercises. No doubt some state commission had found that children were growing up stooped, or with curved spines! They needed more exercise! Every so often, therefore, we stood in neat rows outside the school and, with Miss Rivers demonstrating, obeyed the nasal commands coming from the little Victrola. It was great fun.

Once I caught a butterfly and brought it to school. "Oh, dear, I have no idea what its name is. But I'll bring you a book tomorrow." The book was W. J. Holland's *Handbook of Butterflies*. Overnight I became an amateur lepidopterist. He told exactly how to make a net, mounting boards, and a killing jar. The first items were fairly easy, from things around the house and my mother's help at the sewing machine. The killing jar required some plaster of paris and a chemical I hadn't heard of—potassium cyanide. I made a little shopping list for my mother the next time she went to Poulnot's drugstore. As she reported it, the conversation with the pharmacist went something like this:

"Have you some plaster of paris?"

"Yes, ma'am. How much do you want?"

She consulted her list. "Two or three ounces."

"It comes in pound packages, ma'am—but it's not expensive," he added when my mother hesitated.

He turned to get the plaster of paris and my mother called out, "and two or three ounces of potassium cyanide."

He stopped as if he had walked into a glass wall. Without turning, he said, "What did you say, ma'am?"

"Potassium cyanide."

He came toward her, eyeing her intently.

"Lady, what do you want it for?"

"I don't. My son wants it."

"How old is he?"

"Ten. He wants it to kill butterflies."

"Lady, it will do just that, and probably kill him and his brothers and sisters at the same time! It's one of the most powerful poisons known. I can't sell it without special permission from the state."

I never learned exactly what my mother answered, but when

she recovered, the druggist tried to be helpful. "Why don't you get him to use dry cleaning fluid?"

I was disappointed not to have potassium cyanide. Holland had said in his little book that other poisons—poured on cotton in the bottom of the jar—could be used, but he did not recommend them.

I argued with my mother. "The beauty of potassium cyanide," I was quoting Holland, "is that it kills the insect quickly and does not cause the wing muscles to become rigid."

She was unimpressed; the druggist, I felt, had thoroughly indoctrinated her on the subject of potassium cyanide. "I don't care in the slightest," she said, "whether your little butterflies get rigid or not. I just don't want *you* to get rigid!"

Stated in those terms, the argument silenced me.

Lack of the correct poison was not my only departure from Holland's standards. His guide showed insects impaled on pins two inches long, which he called mounting pins. I used common straight pins. His pictures showed butterflies in wooden, glass-covered boxes with a cork floor. I used shoe boxes and candy boxes to which I had glued slices of bottle corks for holding my pins. Holland portrayed the well-equipped collector with a kind of knapsack slung over his shoulder for jaunts afield, in which one carried the cyanide jar, envelopes for holding dead butterflies, notebook, pencil, and a field glass. My knapsack was my home-made gingham book bag, suspended by a strap diagonally across my chest, but it was sufficient for my jar of damp cotton, envelopes, and Holland's guide.

Butterfly collecting was one of the more durable hobbies that I moved in and out of in those preadolescent years. I roamed the fields of the Lawton plantation with my net, and collected nearly thirty species—the number, I learned later, at which amateur collectors usually stop. Lunging about pasture fields with my big white net, I threw the cows into a panic and mystified the black workers. My brother told me they kept asking him what I was up to. "They think you're nutty," he told me. "They think you should be put in the net."

Ultimately I took my collection to school, where Miss Rivers put it on display for a few days. Then came winter, and my stack of shoe boxes was put away. Then also came the little black ants. I had not seen that thin wavering black line that led from the back of my bureau to a crack in the floor. For several weeks they had been busy. One day when I decided to take a look, I found all the wings had dropped to the bottom of the boxes, and the little bodies were hollow shells. So ended my career as a lepidopterist. If I had used potassium cyanide as I was supposed to do, I told my parents, this would probably not have happened.

If Martha Rivers looked over her shoulder at history, it was not in self-pity or with any wish to hold off tomorrow; it was only in appreciation. With her there could be little longing for the good old days. Educationally, she was as contemporary as the morning paper. If Walter Camp's exercises would be good for us, we would have Walter Camp! She started a Girl Scout troop and a PTA which soon raised enough money to buy two seesaws for the playground. A group of mothers were persuaded to serve hot soup and sandwiches twice a week. She signed up for the Charleston Museum's traveling exhibits of birds and mammals, and a traveling box of books. She entered our art work in the annual Charleston County Fair. In the spring we presented an operetta. And we had a field day!

Surely a middle-aged, maiden lady could say in honesty, "Saturday is my day. I don't have to take a bunch of fifth, sixth, and seventh graders to a track meet." But she did take us, and for a month before, during recesses and after school, we got ready for it. Stiles Bee, a son of one of James Island's planters and a student at Clemson College, decided one spring to take a semester off. Martha Rivers promptly enrolled him as coach at James Island Grammar School. He taught us elementary football, and how to dig toeholds for a foot race, even rehearsing us with a pistol that actually fired. There was broad jumping, high jumping, basketball throw for girls, and shotput for boys. Finally, late in May, we had an all-day meet with Johns Island and Wadmalaw. The winner? James Island Grammar School.

Miss Rivers played the reed organ in the St. James Episcopal Church, and it was hard work. A reed organ works on a vacuum; wind is sucked in over the little reeds, not blown as in pipe organs. A wooden arm stuck out from the side of the organ, and a boy could grasp it and work the bellows to produce the suction. But Martha Rivers preferred to pump the bellows with her feet. She played, slightly bent from the waist, swaying a little from side to side, not unlike a bicyclist pedaling up a hill. Part of her problem was leakage from the bellows. We could hear it as a sort of quiet gasp, especially when she worked up a strong suction to handle the responses between the commandments. We sang, "Lord have mercy upon us and incline our hearts to keep this law" ten times, and she had to be ready.

Miss Jo Seabrook, organist at the Presbyterian church, which we attended on the first, third, and fifth Sundays of each month, confronted no such problems. She sat on the playing-stool composed and erect, mistress of her instrument. There were no leaks in her bellows, and once she got the suction up, she sat there calm and poised, her ankles working rhythmically and took us "Safely Through Another Week" like a swan in full motion.

Martha Rivers's forebears had been planters for at least three generations before her on the plantation known as Secessionville. Cecilia Lawton in 1866 had written in her diary about the refugees returning to James Island after the Union occupation: "I never saw a white woman's face from month to month—for very few had returned from their refugee homes at that time. I heard that some ladies had returned to Secessionville—six miles off—but they had no means of visiting me. No one could then afford the pleasures of horses or vehicles. William Hinson and Elias Rivers, who were then planting on the Island, were almost the only visitors we had."

Martha Rivers was the daughter of Elias Rivers, a captain in the Confederate army. St. James Episcopal Church had been their church, and it was the one I attended on alternate Sundays. It was a little Gothic structure, made of wood with an interior of highly polished tongue-and-groove boards. It looked and felt like a church. The bond with the past was stronger here than with the Presbyterians—or at least I felt it so. It may have been the liturgy and the timeless expressions in the Book of Common Prayer that linked me to history in a way that the Presbyterians could not.

Almighty God, our heavenly father, in whose hands are the living and the dead; we give thee thanks for all those thy servants who have laid down their lives in the service of our country. Grant to them thy mercy and the light of thy presence, that the good which thou hast begun in them may be perfected through Jesus Christ, our Lord.

I think that I knew the things Martha Rivers was remembering as she heard these prayers, and I found myself remembering them, too. Somehow I felt that I belonged in this procession of history; I could even be proud to step up and take my place.

Almighty God who hast given us this good land for our heritage; we humbly beseech thee that we may always prove ourselves a people mindful of thy favor and glad to do thy will. Bless our land with honourable industry, sound learning, and pure manners . . .

There was a certain cold Sunday morning in Advent. This was not Christmas Sunday, when everyone turned out and the church was warm, and there was an overflow choir. It was a day when someone had forgotten to start a fire, and that task had just fallen to the first comer. The little group who gathered for Sunday school that morning kept their coats on and shivered. At ten o'clock Miss Rivers started up the organ with "O Little Town of Bethlehem, How Still We See Thee Lie." I whispered to the boy beside me that I *thought* I was getting a steam engine for Christmas. Then we sang "The First Noel" and huddled around the stove for our Sunday school class. Miss Rivers stopped by to say that she was counting on us for the choir, and went off to a back room to lay out the robes.

Why did they do it—Miss Rivers, my Sunday school teacher, and the people who shivered on that Sunday in Advent? Was it an unthinking response to "the pressures of ancient folkways"? A little exercise that made them feel better—but still an exercise in futility? If that was so, why do I remember it?

I know why now, and I did then. The reason was never uttered—it didn't have to be; we knew without being told. They did it for us.

# 18

# Find Your Calling

"What will you do when you grow up?" In our house one an-swer was obvious; neither I nor my brother could follow in our father's business, for he was a plantation manager—one of a kind—and there were for his job no rights of succession. Help for the likes of us through vocational counseling and career education was unknown in the Charleston County schools of those days. The absence of professional help did not mean, however, that my parents and teachers left career choice to whim and circumstance. I sense now that they were nudging me first in this direction and then another, all the while sending up trial balloons to see which way my preferences might blow them.

I did not sense then that my mother, despite her genuine wish to be submissive to the Divine Will, was at heart ambitious—a bit of a pusher. After one of her visits to school, for example, I found myself moved from the second to the third grade. I had not been kept busy enough. Although she never "stood over us" while we did our homework, as mothers of my friends did, she knew whether Mary Williams got a higher mark than I did, and her comment invariably was, "I certainly wouldn't let that little Mary Williams beat me."

"It doesn't matter how little you are if you're smart," I would reply.

Mary was probably the brightest person in the class, but she was fragile and given to head colds. She always worked with a pencil in one hand and a handkerchief in the other.

"She always beats me in spelling."

"Well, of course, your father can't spell sickum." For genetic reasons I was apparently excused from spelling. "But," she continued, "there is a lot more to school beside spelling. If I were a big strong boy like you, I certainly wouldn't let her beat me. I would just dig in and work harder."

"If I go fast, I'm not neat. She always gets extra points for neatness." A weak argument that got me nowhere.

I was never able to correct my mother's curious belief that there was a positive correlation between vigorous health and the ability to outsmart Mary Williams.

There were two things that I could do rather well—talk in public and play the piano. I wish I could say that I excelled in some group or individual sport; such a proficiency would have added greatly to my self-confidence and social skills. There was no opportunity whatever on James Island for team sports; and as for individual sports, there was swimming, but that was so much a part of our daily lives that it was no more a sport than walking.

The two things that I could do well, however, did not escape the observant eyes of my parents and teachers. Certainly these skills contained vocational possibilities, and I was given ample opportunity to try them out. I would be either a musician or a preacher.

First, there was the matter of music lessons, by which my family meant piano lessons. My maternal grandfather, a farmer, had only rudimentary instruction in reed organ, but he played well enough to give himself and others pleasure, and was a gifted singer. My mother remembers that during her growing-up years he spent Sunday afternoons in the parlor, playing and singing hymns. He was the first in his area to acquire a piano; it was assumed that his children and grandchildren would study long enough "at least to play hymns and help out at church." Soon after our arrival on James Island, therefore, my parents purchased a secondhand piano from Jordan's Music Store. My sister started first, as a pupil of one of the junior teachers in the Cappelmann School of Piano in Charleston. I became immediately fascinated by the keyboard and the sounds it could produce, especially if I played with my sister. Our almost overnight success with "I love coffee, I love tea" and "Chopsticks" must have aroused in my parents the exciting possibilities of concert duet-playing, for in a few weeks I was sent for lessons to my sister's teacher.

The beginning was not auspicious; the discipline of the printed score and the weekly composition to be prepared were the antithesis of the freewheeling I had enjoyed and continued to enjoy. At almost every practice session, I would hear my mother's voice float in from the kitchen over the music I was making. "That doesn't sound like the lesson to me." I was growing hostile toward my teacher; my poor preparation, and my inability to carry out the teacher's directions, made me appear stubborn. I had never heard the piano called "the keyboard," and one day when my teacher said for the third time, voice rising, "Find B flat on the keyboard!" I began to cry. The end was clearly in sight.

Then came Helene T. Kreamer to join the Cappelmann teaching staff, young, pretty, fresh from Leipzig Conservatory with an intriguing German accent. I was assigned to her, and loved her at first sight. She told my parents, "Ooh, he has talent—so much talent," and she gave me a piece called "Song of the Drum," full of strong chords and a brisk rhythm. Helene Kreamer stayed in Charleston only a year, but it was long enough to get me off dead center. I made history with "Song of the Drum." I was a sensation at Christian Endeavor, PTA, school chapel, and church dinners.

The need for program material at such functions was acute, and performers were scarce. No one had to ask me twice for "Song of the Drum." It never occurred to me, in the intoxication of my performance, that the same long-suffering families attended all these functions.

My knack for showy playing and improvisation, and the necessity of preparing a piece for the spring and winter recitals, conspired to short-circuit any genuine training in the fundamentals of music. When it came to polishing off a piece for an upcoming recital, everything else took second place.

By the Circular Congregational Church on Meeting Street in Charleston there was a small masonry building, set well back from the sidewalk, that was known to us as "The Musical Art Club Hall." Here the Cappelmann School of Piano held its recitals. The auditorium on the upper floor was a long, narrow, rectangular room, almost starkly plain; its wide center aisle led to the platform where a black grand piano, cover up, commanded the room. The theory behind the frequent recitals seems to have been that one learns to memorize and perform a piece for an audience only by actually doing so. There would be no carrying a sheet of music to the piano, following the score with bobbing head, turning pages. Never! When your name was called, you walked up to the piano and sat down as if you knew what you were doing—and played. The anxiety level, both for performers and for parents, was intense. A bath in the late afternoon, meticulous scrubbing of fingers, a last-minute running over the piece which probably picked up errors with each repetition, and off to Charleston in the early twilight. We turned onto Cannon Street, where children were playing skip rope and marbles—laughing, carefree. I longed to change places with any one of them. But no; the old Dodge was advancing steadily and relentlessly toward the Musical Art Club Hall.

The evenings usually came off better than we feared. In drilling us for the recital, Miss Cappelmann knew what she was doing. As we became more proficient players, our position on the program moved closer toward the end. To be last of all the performers was a most coveted honor. I never made it. I worried often about wrong notes, but rarely about forgetting, because I had assured myself that whatever happened, I could keep going—I would make it up as I went along. One night, near the end of the program, I returned to my seat to a burst of applause that startled me. It continued for some time after I was seated. This had never happened before, and it sounded good to me. I looked around at the beaming faces. Had I looked more carefully, I would have noticed that Miss Cappelmann's face was scarlet and a little blotched, as she stood waiting for the applause to stop. The evening ended happily for me; a great many people wanted to shake my hand as we stood around the punch bowl. Miss Cappelmann, I learned years later, was having problems right then with professionalism and human relations. She told my parents later that the first half of my piece was "Perpetual Motion"; the last half was nothing she had ever heard before. After all the enthusiastic applause, she hated to confront me with this; the wisest course, she decided, was to have me drop the piece forever and say nothing. I was glad to put "Perpetual Motion" behind me.

In those days rural people had to make their own entertainment; it was the time of readings and recitations—my second strong point. Indeed, any child on James Island who could be wheedled into reciting a poem would surely appear at the next function at the Agricultural Hall. Even though my parents were doubtless gratified at the skills their children could display, there was for them a justification beyond parental show-off for some of the things their children did in public. The Bible contained clear teachings about people using the abilities God had given them. We heard serious talk at home about how we should respond when some adult—the word *adult* was emphasized—asked us to play, whether at school, church, or home. We were not to back away in confusion, "as if you don't know anything." We were to be ready if asked. For a few years, therefore, any hard-pressed program committee chairman on James Island could safely count on a recitation or a piano solo from the Bresee family.

I was never aware of any direct pressure on me to become a minister; no one ever sat down and had a serious conversation with me on the subject. Good Presbyterians believed that one was called to be a minister; indeed, in Christian Endeavor we were taught that every person had a vocation which with God's help one should find. Even so my mentors were deftly arranging my days so that I could pick up the call, should it come. A number of educational and leadership meetings came my way which I now suspect did not appear by chance.

One such meeting was a statewide conference for "early teens" to be held on the campus of Presbyterian College in Clinton, South Carolina. The pamphlet describing the affair stated that many junior high youths lost interest in the church, and this con- ference was to help them "maintain a vision of service." Mary Wil- liams and I were to represent James Island. By now she was no longer my rival, but the girl I asked most often to dance with me at parties at the gin house. An idyllic week it was, of campfires, Bible studies, games, long quiet talks, and dreams. We each fell in love with someone else and came home starry-eyed, a little sad, and with a treasured book of addresses. For a year I wrote letters to a girl in Summerton whose name I can't now remember.

All these propitious circumstances did not produce the desired effect; deep down inside I found myself withdrawing from the prospect of either music or the ministry. Was it the absence of a role model? I did not know a minister whose life-style I wished to emulate, although we would go to the city occasionally for an evening service, to hear some famous preacher. Possibly because of their remoteness, their careers never appeared possible to me.

In one of the city churches a young man who played the grand piano with the pipe organ during the hymn singing came nearer than anyone else to being a role model. We would sit in the balcony directly over the piano, and as he swung into the great chords of "When the Roll Is Called Up Yonder" I resolved that someday I would have those chords flowing from my shoulders and fingertips as they did from his. I attained that goal; it did not require following a score precisely, as long as the general effect was right. I was good at "general effects." A career in music was steadily receding from the field.

To be a preacher? The idea remained dormant. While I knew there would be acceptance and support for such a choice, I was never urged in that direction. My parents, mystics that they were, believed in the "still small voice"; when and if it came, its authority and meaning would be unmistakable.

But the question, "What will you do when you grow up?" grew in intensity as the months passed, as, indeed, it does with all youth. The Christian Endeavor Society never let the urgency of this question leave us. There was a calling for each—our vocation—and with God's help we must find it. That calling, we were taught, was inextricably linked with the needs of the world. Where was that need most acute? In the foreign mission field.

The Christian Endeavor Society met in homes on Sunday evenings, since meeting in the church would mean the lighting of kerosene lamps and possibly a fire. A map of Korea or Brazil would be hung on the wall, along with pictures of children in distant lands who had walked more miles to church than we had ridden in a car. And there were things that boys and girls in America could do to help. The missionaries needed old razor blades, picture postcards, and pencils. We couldn't buy pencils, but we could collect razor blades and cards and turn them in at every meeting. We had a few lessons on home missions, but they were not our chief concern.

The ladies in our little society unflinchingly set before us a demand and an example. The untaught, unconverted masses on those maps were our responsibility, and they would see to it that the boys and girls on James Island did their bit. We must study and give and pray, and the sponsors of Christian Endeavor systematically set about to show us how.

From her bulging handbag on Sunday morning, Mrs. King would draw a sheaf of clippings, each piece bearing a child's name. Passing them out to us, she would say, "Look this over before you come tonight and read it at Christian Endeavor." I would find myself, along with my friends, reading an anecdote from the mission field, or a brief exposition of some theme from the Bible. And so the meeting went. She talked and we talked, and at the end she passed out sentence prayers for us to read as we stood in a circle with our heads bowed. Brazil? Korea? Our prayers could leap the miles. We were part of a grand design.

One Sunday evening Mrs. King said, "I didn't bring any sentence prayers tonight. Let's stand in a circle and you make your own sentence prayer." Our first fumbling attempts. God blessed the missionaries in China and Korea and Brazil many times that night, but we made it around the circle.

In retrospect, I find it hard to fault the twofold emphasis of that little society—to find a calling that would be deeply satisfying personally and acceptable to our Creator, and to direct it toward the betterment of the world.

There was a little song—Mrs. King called it a song of consecration—that often ended our meetings:

I'll go where you want me to go, I'll be what you want me to be . . .
But if, by the still small voice He calls to paths that I do not
   know . . .
I'll go, Dear Lord, with my hand in thine. . . .


A half mile down the King's Highway from our church stood another Presbyterian church—the one for Negroes. It must have had a Sunday school twice the size of ours, if one could judge from the number of children who clustered around its doors. I was never inside. Anyhow, they probably weren't Presbyterians in the true sense; they must have belonged to some division of their own. Their little church looked needy, but they had their own way of doing things, and it was best not to bother them. Our church had a Department of Home Missions that worked with the poor up in the Kentucky mountains. We received pictures for our bulletin board of thin-faced children with big, dark eyes standing in the doorways of weather-beaten houses. Behind each house there was always a steep, wooded hillside. Several times a year our Christian Endeavor had a "Home Missions Sunday" when we would round up a bundle of cast-off clothing, old hymnbooks, and toys for these mountain people. A few weeks later Mrs. King would pass around a letter written in a child's laborious scrawl thanking "the young people for their gifts." That night in our prayer circle, the impoverished children of the Kentucky mountains would share in our request for God's blessing on the world, along with the struggling missionaries in the foreign field. I can't remember that the children from the gray, windowless cabins on James Island ever made it to our little circle of bowed heads.

## 19

# *His Face Has a Good Look*

Supper was over and we had spread our school books on the dining room table, ready to begin our homework. The gasoline lamp, emitting its soft, incessant hiss, flooded us with brilliant white light. My father stood in the doorway, stirring a saucepan of candy.

"We're getting a new storekeeper tomorrow," he said casually. "Mr. Lawton has found a boy who he thinks can do the job."

"A boy?" someone asked.

"Well, a young man. He's in his twenties. Came to the city a few days ago on a tramp steamer. Says he's an able-bodied seaman, but wouldn't mind quitting ship for a shore job. His captain is willing to release him because the boat's going to be in dry dock for quite a while."

"What's his name?"

"Charlie Mack," my father replied.

"That's a funny name."

"I think he might have shortened it from something hard to pronounce."

"What's he look like?" my sister asked.

"How would I know? I haven't seen him."

"Funny, Mr. Lawton just sending him over here," my mother said, half to herself.

In retrospect, I see a shifting set of circumstances which seemed predetermined to fall into the precise pattern that brought Charlie to the Lawton plantation toward the close of our stay on James Island. If the tramp steamer *Doric Star* had not developed engine trouble and put into Charleston dry-dock for repairs; if Charlie had not, in boredom and loneliness, gone that evening to the Seamen's Home; if he had not had a long talk with the Reverend Stanley Martin, chaplain of the home; if the Reverend Martin had not also been Alison Lawton's pastor at St. James Church; if Lemuel Knight, our storekeeper, had not that week decided to return to his little farm near Jamestown . . .

"Well," my mother persisted, "do we know anything about his background—who he is?"

"Reverend Martin got to know him at the Seamen's Home and took a liking to him. That's the place the Episcopal church runs to be a sort of 'home-away-from-home' for sailors who don't want to spend all their time in those taverns on East Bay. Martin admits he doesn't know a lot about him, but he's sure this Mack fellow isn't just run-of-the-mill, and he asked Mr. Lawton if there wasn't some work for this Charlie on the plantation. Lem's last day is Saturday and we'll need someone in the store. Mr. Lawton asked me to give him a try. We'll have to wait and see."

"Maybe he's gotten fed up with the ocean already," my mother said. "You read about so many boys who get upset over something and rush off to sea—and then regret it."

"Martin's sure he's O.K.," my father said. "All preachers seem to think they can tell if a man is any good—they have some intuition, inner prompting—or something."

"I suppose he'll live in that little cottage by the creek?"

"Yes, he says he's not a bad cook. The room has an oil stove, a sink, and a decent bed. Mr. Lawton called his captain. He says the boy was a good seaman, always did his job, and got along well with the rest of the crew. As I said, we'll have to wait and see."

"When's he coming?"

"Tomorrow on the noon boat."

I have wondered since if Charlie ever looked back and asked himself how, of all the jobs he might have found in the Charleston area, he happened to take the one on the Lawton plantation.

School was still in session, or I would have been down at the wharf the next day to meet the noon boat; as it was, I had to be content with my father's account of his arrival.

"What's he look like?"

"He's in his early twenties, medium height, has light hair. He's a good-looking young fellow, and seems pretty intelligent. When I went out to the end of the wharf to get the mailbag, he jumped off and helped Sam tie up—as if he knew boats.

"He put his hand out and said he was Charlie Mack and asked me how I pronounced my name. He had a big bag with him that I asked Ned to put in the cart and drop it off at the little house where he'll stay. We went into the store and met Lem. Charlie said he'd be willing to start in this afternoon and learn the ropes, since Lem's leaving soon. I liked him. He has a good clean-cut appearance." That was my father's expression for a young man who impressed him as serious and promising. My mother would later confer on Charlie her favorite accolade for a young man she thought bright and honorable, "His face has a *good* look."

After school the next day I went down to the store to find out about the new man for myself. Lem was opening cartons and Charlie was stacking cans of vegetables on a shelf. Lem introduced me.

"This is Clyde. He's the boss's oldest boy." Charlie smiled and said "hello" and kept on working.

"My father said you are from Baltimore."

"Well, not really *in* Baltimore—but near there."

"A little town?"

"Yeah, pretty small—you wouldn't have heard of it." He did not stop working, and I got the impression that I should not pursue the subject of his origins any further.

"We came from Pennsylvania—northern part," I said.

"Yeah? Nice state. I've never been there." He was climbing down off the stepladder. "Mr. Knight, where do you want all this salt pork put?"

"We call that butts-meat down here, my boy. It should go in the bottom of the icebox. And that's another job you will have— keeping ice in that thing. You can get it up at the dairy and bring it down with John and the cart. He's always wandering around here somewhere. And, sir, I want to tell you something." He put down the sugar scoop he was using in a special effort to be sociable. "That John is the smartest mule on James Island—or anywhere. I've farmed all my life, and I've never seen anything like him. We let him wander around the place with the cart behind him, and when he hears our boat coming around the bend in the creek, he'll come right down here all by himself and back the cart up to the wharf to get the empty milk cans. Do you suppose he mixes up our boat with those going to the public wharf? Not on your life! Well, you can take him to get the ice."

As he instructed Charlie, Lem Knight—like many men with simple, routine jobs—did his best to make his work sound complex and important.

"Watching out for the mail is your job. If Mr. Bresee isn't here, you get that bag—it's an old leather saddle bag—and bring it to the store and keep it safe behind the counter. Don't let the boy in the boat throw it up to you—make him hand it to you."

Charlie took a little pad out of his pocket and made notes as Lem talked. I thought, "Charlie's taking this job seriously."

As my father had predicted, Charlie did work out "all right." A clerk in the Lawton plantation store was not engaged in competitive selling; the workers from our end of the island could obtain their simple needs at our store or go without. On the other hand, we would not tolerate a clerk who was lordly or arrogant in dealing with the blacks. Charlie's response was instinctively open and courteous; he could smilingly ask a customer to interpret for him a request made in Gullah dialect, and then carry on without a trace of condescension.

He fitted into the routine of the plantation, and yet he did not fit. He opened the store on time and kept it far neater than had Lem Knight, his sales were high, he was cooperative and dependable, yet there was always a reserve that even I could feel. The white men of the plantation would often gather at the store a few minutes before the noon boat arrived, to wait for their mail. They might lounge on the porch, or against the great exposed roots of the water oaks that overshadowed the store, and drink a bottle of soda while they waited for our boat to come around the bend in the creek. Charlie would have a soda, too, listen to their talk and laugh with them, but always as an agreeable spectator. I suppose he could hardly have been expected to enter a conversation on cows freshening, corn crops, sweet potatoes, and velvet beans.

I see now that he was probably lonely, but too proud to reveal it. Our family made their usual minimal overtures of friendship, an invitation to supper, an invitation to church, and inquiries about his family and background—inquiries that elicited from Charlie a disappointingly small store of information. He had "lived around" with aunts and uncles part of his life, was glad to leave a small town—"you wouldn't have heard of it"—and be out "on my own." One gained the impression that this superficial account of his beginnings was all he was going to report for now. Yes, he liked the South, was terribly glad to have a job at the Bluff. Everyone had been friendly—especially the Negro customers.

"I can't get used to having everyone call me 'Mr. Mack' all the time," he said. "I told them 'Charlie was O.K.' Then one of them said, I think it was the boy Jamsie, 'How 'bout us call you Mistuh Charlie?' I told him that was O.K., too."

"They know old James Island customs better than you do," my father said smiling. "There's a kind of etiquette—maybe that's not the word for it—here on these islands that is different. Mr. Lawton told me about it before we decided to come here to live. We get along with the Negroes here differently than they do even fifty miles upstate."

"I'm really glad to be on this old plantation," Charlie replied. "I'm getting a good education in local history, too."

My mother returned to the matter of church. "We'd love to have you visit our church some Sunday. You could ride with us, if you like."

I didn't like the idea at all. I couldn't imagine Charlie on his way to Sunday school squeezed into the back seat of the blue Dodge with the Bresee children. I was relieved when he announced other plans. But my mother had tried.

"I think I'll drop in at the Seamen's Home on Sundays for a while," he told her. "I know a few people there, and I can get a ride over on the morning boat."

Though Charlie and the Bresees were both Northerners, I never felt that this fact created any bond between us. Our lives now were full, and as the summer days passed, any social advances that we made became more and more perfunctory because he needed us less. As the storekeeper, Charlie joined the white men who worked for my father: John Posey, supervisor of field work and maintenance, and S. M. Tucker, who was in charge of pasteurization. Each carried on his work effectively and with remarkably good will, as far as I could observe. The harmony among the four men who ran the plantation doubtless had much to do with the satisfaction I found in living on the Bluff. Whether at school or in the city, I was always undergirded by a quiet sense of anticipation at the thought of being back among them again. I would return to fields and trees and marshlands whose beauty and fascination I detected and loved even as a child, but better still, I would return to people who liked each other. Charlie, though the last to join these men and bearing always a faint reserve, did his part loyally and became one of them—up to the day of his precipitous departure.

## 20

# *Across the Ashley*

Even as a child I sensed that James Island was Queen of the Sea Islands. It had everything. I used to feel sorry for the people stuck back on Wadmalaw or Edisto—or even our big neighbor, Johns Island. They had good plantations, wide water ways, groves of live oaks, and nice homes, but they never could "get anywhere." By anywhere, I meant the city of Charleston. They were so far from town, whereas on James Island I had two worlds—the fascinating world of the tidelands, and the excitement of Charleston, a half mile away across the river "as the crow flies."

There was much about Charleston in those days that was ugly and frightening, but I was unaware of it. We did not explore the slum area or worry much about social problems. Charleston meant to me the beautiful skyline on the peninsula and the busy harbor, both of which I saw daily from my bedroom window. It also meant the Charleston Museum, music lessons, Bullwinkle's Bakery, Woolworth's Five and Ten, and Saturday afternoons at the Majestic Theater.

I went from one world to the other in a twinkling. Roads of sand or clay, edged by arching trees and hedgerows, wound through cultivated fields and came at length to the new concrete bridge over the Ashley; then a turn onto Chinquapin Street and you were in the city.

Music lessons on Tuesday and Saturday were my chief occasions for regular visits to Charleston. School dismissal at two o'clock

found my mother waiting in the Dodge touring car, ready for the trip to town. She brought our music, sandwiches, apples, and two wet washcloths. My poor mother was never satisfied with the state of our hands, but one can do only so much with a wet washcloth. She left us at the studio of W. Gertrude Cappelmann, 200 Rutledge Avenue, scrubbed and combed to the extent possible in the back seat of a moving car.

W. Gertrude Cappelmann—music teacher, second-generation German, staunch Lutheran. Could anyone doubt that the first initial stood for Wilhelmina? She was also the founder and principal of the Cappelmann School of Piano.

This organization was actually a consortium of eight teachers who gave private piano lessons. They were banded together under Gertrude Cappelmann's leadership, in a way I never fully understood. She presided at all recitals, developed a system of certificates, diplomas, and award pins, and wrote all the publicity. As pupils we realized that she was the boss, had most of the better pupils, and charged the highest fees.

She was an administrator and promoter of the first order. She knew what the public wanted and how to deliver it. I have heard my parents remark on her dignified and commanding presence at recitals, a presence due in no small part to the magnificent gowns that she wore. An erect, large woman, she would walk slowly to the front of the hall, turn and stand smiling a moment before she spoke, as if giving everyone an opportunity to admire the brocaded dress and perfect coiffure. She knew instinctively that parents wanted good theater and were willing to pay for it. She announced the youngest beginner's solo by title and composer without a trace of condescension. When a little boy or girl walked up to the big black piano to play a first recital piece, the audience would be treated to two full minutes of concertizing.

A program of beginning and "medium" players can be tiring

even to an audience of doting relatives, but Gertrude Cappelmann's sense of sound teaching knew how to handle that. Toward
the end of the program she might say, "Is Miss Fowler or Mr.
Weston in the audience?" She knew they were; they were her advanced pupils. Speaking with great dignity to these people who
might not be there, she would continue, "Before you go back to
your studies at the College of Charleston, would you play for us?"

Youthful and confident, one or the other of them would come
smiling up the aisle and sit down at the piano. Then for the first
time in our lives we would be in the presence of playing that approached the professional level. Was this the same piano? Were we
still in the same room? I heard here, for the first time in my life,
the great Chopin Polonaise and the "Aeolian Harp" Etude. Fine
phonographs and fine recordings did not exist then; we would
hear this music in concert performance or not at all. It was not
just the poise and self-assurance of the players, or the accuracy of
their flying fingertips that dazed us; it was the music itself. So this
was what it was all about! Music was no longer merely a tune you
could play and hum, or some clever tricks that impressed your
friends. It was a journey right out of this world. Can any experience match the impact of a Liszt Hungarian Rhapsody happening
for the first time, on a grand piano within ten feet of you?

Then the music went back into the silent printed notes with no
way it could be heard again—unless—unless—maybe one of us
could work hard enough . . . Miss W. Gertrude Cappellmann, indeed, understood sound teaching as well as good showmanship.

There would be one last try to make me a musician. A re-
nowned New York teacher and pianist, Leslie Hodgson, was offering a six-week Master Course in Charleston during the summer.
Miss W. Gertrude Cappellmann convinced my parents that he was
what my floundering talent needed. I would be the only child he
would take. There would be two lessons a week at a total cost of

$120, a sum that would have been unthinkable had not my mother just inherited $1,000 from her father's estate. I remember the morning that we drove to Charleston to withdraw the money. My mother had probably never handled such a sum in her life. Her cheeks were flushed and her face tense when she came from the bank and drove at once to the Musical Art Club Hall. I think she was afraid we would be "held up."

Mr. Hodgson stood smiling by the grand piano, took the money and gave her a receipt.

The Master Course was felicitous, but on the whole unproductive. My proclivity to stray from the printed score was incurable. If there was a flowing left-hand accompaniment of broken chords, I would change the notes daily, unaware that I had done so until Mr. Hodgson corrected me. I understood years later that he said I had a remarkable imagination, played with great expression, had a strong musical sense, but doubted that I ever could follow a printed score. Time has proved him right.

Eight grand pianos on a flower-decked stage—each played by one of the teachers of the Cappelmann School of Piano! This was the scene at the gala commencement that Gertrude Cappelmann staged one June evening in the auditorium of the High School of Charleston. The ensemble opened the program with a sequence of pieces showing a pupil's growth from beginner to accomplished performer—all arranged and directed by W. Gertrude Cappelmann. As the eight teachers left the stage, a big piano was pushed forward, and ten pupils who would play solos in the second section of the program came down the aisle to take their places at the front of the auditorium. Sitting in the balcony, my parents watched my sister and me perform in this group. Then there was a flurry of presentations—awards, certificates, and diplomas. The pianos were rearranged, the eight performers took their places,

Miss Cappelmann raised her baton, and a crashing march ended the program.

Could anyone who attended that concert ever doubt that Miss Gertrude Cappelmann's fee for lessons was worth every cent she charged?

She was a good administrator and a kind of impresario, but Gertrude Cappelmann was also my teacher, and it is as such that I remember and honor her. I see now that she must have been puzzled to distraction by my idiosyncrasies. Beneath her demands and assignments I sensed as all children can—if it be present—that quality of personal caring which characterizes all good teaching.

My musical talent was not so strong that I was automatically attracted to the great German masters that she loved. They had to be prescribed, line by line. I could play chords that brought people forward in their chairs, but spinning out a long run in Bach or Mozart was not my métier. We would plod for months through a Clementi sonata, but she knew that I would have "Turkish March from the Ruins of Athens" ready in two weeks. Gertrude Cappelmann let me be the confirmed romantic that I was, and would wait for another day to teach me Bach.

It was in the spring of my memorable twelfth year that she was asked to "bring some talent" to the State Education Convention in Greenville. She chose an advanced college student and me—the two ends of the spectrum, as it were. We boarded a Pullman car that had been waiting on a siding; a train would pick us up during the night and we would wake up in Greenville the next morning.

Before the porter made up the berth, Gertrude Cappelmann produced from her luggage a cardboard box firmly tied with string. She placed the box on her lap and began untying the knots. "I always get hungry when I travel," she said. "I thought you boys might, too. Then who knows? The train might get held up."

She passed out sausages, brown bread, deviled eggs, pickles, and black chocolate cake—"a good German lunch," my father remarked when I told my story.

"This is our little visit to the refrigerator before we go to bed," she chuckled. This was a Miss Cappelmann that I had not known before.

We played our pieces in a small auditorium in Greenville, apparently to a seminar or lecture type of meeting. We left immediately after performing and were taken about the city by our host family. Next to actually playing, the most memorable event of the trip, and the one that created the greatest stir at home, had happened on our arrival in the Greenville station. As we descended from the train, Gertrude Cappelmann told us to wait.

"Put down your suitcases, boys. I want a porter to carry your bags."

I protested. I had carried much heavier things than this, I told her.

"One thing that pianists cannot do," she said, "is to grip and lift things with their fingers. The great pianists all know this and they will not carry their luggage. It isn't a matter of being big and strong—it's those little muscles in your hand that must be protected."

I watched self-consciously as a red-capped porter grabbed up our bags and told us to follow him.

Back in Charleston several days later my family met me at 200 Rutledge Avenue, and I began pouring out my story. On the way home my sister asked, "Did you play for seven thousand people? The paper said there would be about seven thousand teachers there."

"No, only for about two hundred, I guess."

My brother in the back seat of the car gave the suitcase a trial lift. "You mean carrying this hurts your hand?" He dropped it disdainfully.

"Did they hire someone to carry your bag *after* you played?" Gladys asked.

"No, I had to carry it myself then."

"Gee, your hand must have hurt awful," my brother said.

When we reached home, I turned to Kenneth in the back seat and said, "You can leave my bags on the front porch."

He opened the rear door of the touring car, pushed my suitcase onto the ground, and as he ran into the house, called over his shoulder, "Nothing doing, Paderewski!"

I did not know it then, but Gertrude Cappelmann suffered from a serious back ailment that had caused her to wear a steel brace for most of her life. In teaching, she always sat to my left as I played. She was usually sitting when I entered the room and sitting when I left, giving her greetings and instructions from a bright up-turned face. Once, at the end of a long lesson I said, in the naïveté and bungling honesty of childhood, "You've just sat there and listened all your life, haven't you?" I wish now that I hadn't said those words. I could not know then that, like all true teachers, she found her life's meaning in the attainment of others. She knew the few grand and luminous moments of the big recitals, when achievement blazed forth for all to see; but most of her life she sat in the big chair by the piano fanning sparks.

After the music lesson on Tuesdays, we were to wait in the Charleston Museum for the return of the blue Dodge. America's oldest museum impressed me as looking the way a museum should look. Gently sloping masonry steps led to a semicircular porch flanked by stone columns. Inside, one was aware of cavernous space covered by a skylight ceiling. Hung in the center, from a roof that apparently had no supports, was the complete skeleton of a fifty-foot whale that had been captured in Charleston harbor. I would wander through the Egyptian section where the toes of a mummy stuck through the wrappings, the skeleton department, the birds and mammals, ending up always in the children's room. Here was a lady who could always answer my questions, and a library. Coming from a home where books were loved but scarce, and a school whose library consisted of two shelves of donated books, I found the children's room an oasis.

We would read and roam until we were gently ushered out of the door at five o'clock. Then a wait on the steps for the blue Dodge to come into view. Sometimes my mother was late. The big doors closed, and the museum workers would hurry down the steps, bidding us a perfunctory goodnight as they went by. The sun, now low in the west, gleamed in the windows of the three-storied houses on Rutledge Avenue, and made soft shadows from the cornices of buildings. I would experience that stab of loneliness so peculiar to cities at sundown, when everyone is hurrying home but you. I was to learn years later that I was not alone; people before me had written of those poignant moments "in the city as the sun sinks low."

Saturdays offered much more excitement. I would leave Miss Cappelmann's studio at about twelve o'clock and head downtown. For a complete afternoon I needed thirty cents, but I could adapt to twenty or even ten cents. In Woolworth's I could find shelves of Horatio Alger books at ten cents apiece; then to the candy counter for chocolate-coated peanuts—ten cents. Then a walk back up King Street to the Majestic Theater where the last dime admitted me to a Western and the next chapter of "the serial."

Other James Islanders often joined me here, and once inside we munched our peanuts and waited expectantly through the piano "pre-lude." The lights went out and we were in the world of Zane Grey and fighter airplanes. The piano rippled and thundered while we chewed and reached blindly for peanuts. The pianist taught me new tricks at almost every performance. There was a furious trill in the bass when a plane took off, and a stunning glissando down the piano when one crashed. I would try out these effects at home for my friends, but I could never get the galloping horses to sound right.

Exciting as the half day in Charleston was, I always relished the ride home. The city did not thin out into a succession of gas stations and run-down buildings; at the edge of the Ashley River it just stopped. Once over the bridge, I was back among the live oaks and pines and quiet roads and the smell of wood smoke. Supper time meant the starting up of a hundred fires. Negroes were hurrying to their homes along the main roads, afoot and in mule carts. The institutionalized poverty all about me did not obscure the joys of evening and of going home. If, indeed, there was a measure of peace in this scene, it was born of day's-end weariness, and the in-gathering of those who need each other at night. The sense of tranquillity could reach out to me even across the social and economic chasm that separated me from the hurrying figures at the roadside.

We were going home—this was our bond—and it did not matter to me how different our homes might be, nor did it matter to me then that I always rode and most of them walked. We did not think to offer one of the tired workers a ride in our car. It would have been awkward and upsetting, in a way that would be hard to put into words—so hard, in fact, that no one that I knew ever tried. There were two life-styles, almost two cultures, and there was a kind of orderliness about it. There could be only confusion

if anyone sought to do any blending; who then would know what to expect? Part of my sense of peace and contentment lay in the orderliness of it all.

A good and satisfying order it was to me then, hunched down in the back of the Dodge touring car trying to read my new Horatio Alger book. When we reached the Bluff, the plowing and hoeing would have been done. Our workers would have gone to their cabins, and smoke would be rising from the chimneys. At our house Azalee, our cook, would have left supper partially prepared before going home for the day. My mother would set it out for us, and Azalee would take care of the dishes in the morning. Supper and homework and the new book to read until bedtime. Stay up as long as you can, because there is no reading in bed with a kerosene lamp.

I would drink in the sights and sounds that poured in through the dormer windows of my bedroom. In that temperate climate windows seemed to be open most of the year. At one was the city and the harbor, and at the other the live oaks in the yard and the plantation sounds. I could stand there and dream and listen, with no fear that someone would snap on the light and ask what I was up to. The wind moving through the little leaves of a live oak makes a soft, delicate sound—quite unlike the rustle of maple leaves that I had heard in Pennsylvania. If the night was quiet, and if I listened very hard, I could hear the surf pounding on Morris Island.

I make no claim to having been more profound or more poetic than other children, and I certainly did not stand every night dreaming at the window sill. Like all children, I was acutely aware of the sights and smells and sounds around me. One does not have to be mature to sense the mystery of the night—stars, tree shadows, tree sounds. There is such a thing as first love. As I heard the stir of the leaves in the great oaks, the barking of a dog in the Negro quarters, and breathed air soft and hazy with the smoke from dying fires, I am certain that I never said, "God, what is the meaning of all this?" I absorbed it simply, wordlessly—as my due—as a child accepts air and sunshine and love . . .

## 21

# *Carolina Moon,*
# *Keep Shining*

The year 1928, my eighth summer at the Bluff, was a steadily expanding delight. I had "graduated" from seventh grade, I could drive a car all over James Island; I was going to little dances in the evening for boys and girls of my own age; I was finding new pleasure in little jaunts and excursions with "our bunch" on Sunday afternoons. It was fun just to talk and look at each other and try to say things that would make a girl laugh. Odd that girls' laughter made you feel so good.

The only gloom on the horizon was the High School of Charleston, come September. The terrors of the place, which were detailed for us with special relish by the older boys, were only partially offset by the new privileges that accrued to one who was "going to high school."

"It's time now that these young people know how to conduct themselves at a party. The boys should learn how to fox-trot and waltz and ask a girl for a dance. They will be going to the High School of Charleston next September." So went the talk among a group of James Island mothers in the early days of that memorable summer.

There might not have been any parties if someone had not thought of the gin house. Obviously fifteen or twenty kids can't have a dance in a living room. The top floor of the gin house at Williams might provide the answer. Cotton production had almost ceased on James Island by the time we arrived, having been wiped out by the boll weevil. The famed long-staple, sea island cotton had not been raised on James Island since World War One, leaving the larger plantations with a big, useless, three-storied building. Raw cotton was collected on the top floor to be fed into the ginning machines below. The ground floor eventually became a mule shed or tool barn, but the top floor stood vacant.

The cotton house at Williams was ideal; it was large enough, had good flooring, could be reached by a set of outside steps. All that had to be done was to string up some electric lights, bring in some chairs for the chaperones, sprinkle some corn meal on the floor, and set a portable Victrola in the corner.

These parties were not affairs that one could drift into, talk to a few girls, and then move on. First, you had to be invited; the mothers were going to do it right. Furthermore, the guests had to be "brought" by adults; no one of our age could drive a car at night. Mothers might remain, if they chose, and help to chaperone the party. These dances were not for casual drop-ins, and especially not for the children from some of the new families that were appearing on the island and whose connections we knew nothing about.

On opening night my sister and I climbed the two flights of stairs, tense with anticipation. Our mother, we were relieved to note, had chosen not to be a chaperone. "Carolina Moon, keep shining—shining on the one who waits for me," floated down to us from the overstrained Victrola. Laughter and music at the top of the stairs—music and girls' laughter. There was a magic here that I could not explain. They in their filmy dresses, smiling down at us; I in my blue flannel coat and light trousers. I fairly leaped up the steps. We gathered on a platform at the top of the stairs that served as a little porch under the stars. We leaned over the rail and talked and laughed—and laughed.

Mrs. Williams came to the door. "Come on in, you-all. It's time for a Paul Jones." Someone changed the record to "Baby Face." We formed a big circle, boy, girl, boy, girl.

"Begin!" Left hand, right hand, left—everybody is smiling. The girls go past me one by one. I think, "If they'd say Paul Jones—NOW—but no, too late." Velma will never make it around again. Suddenly the cry, "Paul Jones!" My hand is touching Sally's hand now and we dance. I can't remember that any hand at that moment would have been a disappointment. The elevated mood of the evening has imbued every smiling girl with glamour, and casts every boy in a courtly role that not one of us will ever belie. The party dresses, the perfume, her warm back beneath my hand, the cautious touch of her breast against my coat lapels. "Baby Face! You've got the cutest little Baby Face." Back and forth over the cornmeal boards we go.

"You're getting so much better," Sally tells me. Girls always saw themselves as teachers and encouragers at these parties. "You are so easy to follow."

Then a pause as a record is changed, and the Victrola rewound. Mrs. Williams is speaking in her deliberate, measured manner. "You know that boys may break in and ask for the rest of the dance. I see that we have a couple of extra boys." She smiles in the direction of two newcomers. "This is your chance, you know."

The music changes. "Two by Two, They Go Marching Through—The Sweethearts on Parade." I think, Isn't anyone going to break in and ask for Sally? If I were free, I could . . . A girl can't turn you down when you break in on the dance floor. You don't actually have to say anything—just a touch on her partner's arm and he has to give her up. It's much safer than crossing the room to a row of girls and picking one out.

Our chaperones knew what they were doing. Lots of "Paul Joneses" and lots of "breaking in" made a good party.


I heard years later that she became Miss Charleston in a beauty contest—that girl who sat ahead of me in James Island school and whose shoulder-length brown hair brushed the pencils in front of me. The desks in the seventh-grade row were crowded—mine touched the back of her chair and I could feel the soft, fragrant tips of her hair on the back of my hand when I reached for a pencil. To this day I cannot smell the scent of Coty's perfume but I am swept back to those moments. When I asked Velma a question she had a way of tipping her head back to hear me better, but not turning. The rich brown hair would fall over my desk, and my hands. I would lean forward to whisper, sit motionless, inhale deeply, trying to sustain the moment forever. A look from Miss Rivers brought me back to work. Such, I was to learn, is the way of first love—the battle against time and separation and the battle lost.

That year I read my first romantic novel. As I have already said, there were so few books available that we read anything we could get our hands on. Somewhere I found a copy of Gene Stratton Porter's *Girl of the Limberlost*. The wise and beautiful Ellenora sat in front of me, and in the pure, adoring love of Phillip I found my counterpart. His love would never falter through all eternity; he would wait for her to be his wife until she was fully ready. How could he find words that so accurately sounded the depths of my own heart?

Of one thing I was quite certain: these laughing, thoughtless boys sitting around me had no conception of the exquisite private world of exultation and longing that I experienced. They even laughed at perfume and called it "stinkum." A whiff of Coty's perfume, a sidelong glance from Velma's dark eyes, her faint smile and the breathtaking tumble of wavy hair on the back of my hand. I knew they wouldn't understand even if I tried to tell them.

Were Oscar and Eddie in love when they talked about girls? It hardly seemed so. Fascinated as I was by their conversation, I found it strangely disquieting. Did they long just to be near someone as I did? And fear, as I did, that she might pay attention to another boy? Sometimes they didn't even seem to speak my language at all. Girls in their world were abundant—they came from all directions; you simply had to choose one and let the others take turns. I had watched their friends in the store on Friday nights. They tickled each other, they almost wrestled, they would walk off in the dark still carrying on. Did Oscar really love Victoria, grabbing at her that way? It was all so confusing.

Eddie was less reticent about his adventures. Eddie was tall and gangling with long arms and big hands, and he let it be known that everything about him was long and big. The girls loved it—or so he said. Of course it was wrong, what he talked about, but absorbing nonetheless. I knew what it was—it was fornication; I had looked it up in the dictionary. Evil though it was, I couldn't put it out of my mind; it was no doubt what the Bible meant by "the pleasures of sin." It was plainly wrong to be attracted to something so evil. After a dozen years in Sunday school I hadn't missed those words about lusting in your heart for something being the same as going out and doing it. But that seemed stupid—how could thinking about a thing be as bad as doing it? Weird logic, that. Something was wrong here. But one thing was plain to see; your lust might be a secret sin, but at least it was *secret,* infinitely preferable to being caught at it, or having some-one talk. The whole matter got so tangled that I put it out of my mind. Or tried to. When I didn't hear the boys at the barn talk about it the problem wasn't so bad.

Could you love a girl in two ways, maybe? Whether one of them was love or not I wasn't sure, but two ways of *thinking* about a girl? Well, my way was definitely better. What I thought about made me feel proud and like writing a poem to Velma if I could. Eddie's and Oscar's talk never made me feel like writing a poem. Whatever they meant by love and did to girls was their business. Of one thing I was sure: what they talked about had nothing to do with how I felt about Velma. My conscience was clear on the matter; I didn't lust after Velma. I just thought she was the most exquisite, warm, beautiful, fragrant girl I knew and when she smiled at me and wrote in my autograph album, "You are my best friend forever," the day was sweet and perfect like nothing I had known before. I wanted my dream of marrying Velma and living happily ever after to come true. Those guys at the barn must be talking about something else.

I suppose Oscar and Eddie talked so much about girls because they didn't have much else to talk about. No world series, no newspaper headlines, no TV programs, no football games, no let-ters from friends, no magazines—only the people you saw every-day and what they told you. For a great many, there was church and Sunday school, where one might get new ideas, and for some there was prayer meeting. But here we are back to girls again. Eddie said Wednesday nights were best, like on the way home from prayer meeting—that was a good time for it. Wednesdays and Sunday nights after church. "Just two nights a week?" I said once with a knowing air. Why did I bait them on like this? If I wasn't supposed to lust, it was kind of fun to see how they lusted.

"Not *just* two," he said defensively. "No man can go out every night, Clyde." I agreed with him emphatically.

Wednesdays and Sundays. That was a useful bit of information. I'd stop in at the barn on Thursdays and Mondays. Like Eddie and Oscar, I went to church on Sunday nights—Christian Endeavor Society—but here the similarity ended, because I rode home in the back seat of the Dodge touring car and they walked. Watching those people having all that fun and freedom along the roadside made me almost wish that I was walking. Oscar could be among those couples I would see disappearing into the hedgerow as our headlights approached.

The carryings-on of my friends at the dairy were not for me, and they might get you into a lot of trouble. At Christian Endeavor we often sang:

> Yield not to temptation
> Dark passions subdue.

There was certainly a connection between what the boys talked about and "dark passions"—no doubt about it. We also sang:

> Shun evil companions
> Bad language disdain.

Did I have any evil companions? Probably, but whatever they told me in Christian Endeavor I was sure of one thing: I would never shun Oscar and Eddie. I wasn't even sure they were that evil—but they sometimes were, sort of.

As for bad language, I didn't use it very often, and when I was with Oscar and Eddie they did most of the talking. I just listened.

Anyhow, tomorrow would be Monday and the thought warmed me. A lot of kids hated Mondays, but I didn't. I could help Velma with her arithmetic, smell the fragrance of her hair and see her smile—it would be a good day. After school, I'd probably come to the barn to talk with Oscar and Eddie awhile. Just out of curiosity. It would be fun to hear how they made out on Sunday night . . .

## 22

# *Charlie Mack*

I heard about Eva and Charlie Mack really by third hand: Eva confided in her sister, Victoria; Victoria told her boyfriend, Oscar Middleton, and Oscar told me. He didn't tell me directly, but allowed me to listen when he talked to Eddie as they worked around the dairy barns. Once he put down a milk pail, looking at me with an intent, anxious face, "Clyde, I sure hope you doan talk 'bout dis to nobody. Dis can make bad trouble fo' a lot of people."

"Oscar," I said, "I promise you I'll never talk about this to anyone—not anyone—never."

"Clyde, I sure be glad if you don't." He turned and carried the pail of milk to the dairy, and I did not speak to him again that evening.

Everyone on the plantation agreed that Evalina Washington was a pretty girl. The Bresee family so described her, and I am sure that many people—men especially—would, far back in their minds, say that Evalina was beautiful. I never heard any of my planter friends in those days describe a black woman as beautiful; she could be nice-looking, cute, or even pretty. Perhaps the word *beautiful* revealed too much about the speaker. It went beyond objective descriptive of a person "out there," and told something about the beholder that, though it be genuine enough, could never on James Island be properly disclosed. Calling a woman beautiful could mean, "I admire you," and the word comes alarmingly close to saying, "I could love you."

Charlie Mack found Evalina beautiful.

I learned about Eva—Oscar and her family used that name—from her older sister, Victoria, Oscar's steady girlfriend. Victoria was warm, convivial, and immensely likable. She bore the alert, earnest air of the eldest daughter who had been required early in life to manage small children. We would see her often about the plantation, fetching a pail of water on her head, minding her brothers and sisters, buying food at the store, and, of course, talking to Oscar whenever she could manage to escape the demands of her family. She walked always with a cheerful bounce that made her full, firm breasts sway invitingly under her thin, sleeveless dresses. I found it easy in my early adolescent years to imagine the pleasures that Oscar might experience alone with Victoria after dark. Yet in spite of her obvious sexuality she was never regarded as a bad girl, or as one who "ran around." She was a good, loving, big sister who, according to Oscar, was worried sick over Eva.

Physically Eva was a diminutive of Victoria, smaller boned, slim, more graceful. The open, inviting face of Victoria had become controlled, dignified and gentle in Eva—the smile shy, the eyes questioning. Eva was a "proper girl," which may have been why many white people called her Evalina, and why the Ravenels of Oyster Point had taken her on as their maid. This unbelievable good fortune meant that Eva now had money for a better dress, good shoes, and new ribbons in her hair. The refining influence of an ordered household, a balanced meal at noon, hearing correct speech were producing changes that only enhanced Eva's natural graces. She possessed a quality that later in my life I would hear ascribed to certain actresses and poets—she had presence.

I can see Eva coming down the road by the marsh in late afternoon carrying her mother's empty oil can. She climbs the steps to the store porch, opens the rickety screen door, notices me on the oat bin, and says with a quick smile, "Hello, Mistuh Clyde." Then to Charlie she holds out the can, "Will you please pump me a gallon of kerosene, Mistuh Mack?" I am sure I did not articulate my thoughts then, but it was pleasant to watch Eva do almost anything—even buy a gallon of kerosene at the plantation store.

The hot August mornings of summer on James Island found me often down at the wharf, especially if the tide was coming in. I loved the waterfront at daybreak. I could catch a few shrimp with the dip net, bait my hooks and fish from the wharf, or push off in a rowboat and fish at the bend of the creek. Going or coming, I would stop to talk with Oscar and Eddie as they did the milking. One morning I arrived as they were washing the cows' udders. I had not actually entered the barn, but was standing outside under a row of open windows, when I heard Eddie say to Oscar, "You *sure* it was Mistuh Mack?"

"Yeah, man. Victoria say she *sure*." I stood still. By staying close to the wall under the windows, I could hear the conversation clearly without being seen.

Oscar was speaking. "Victoria she say to Eva, 'Come on to bed; it's late.' Eva say, 'I ain' so sleepy now an' it's too hot in dere. I tink I set on de steps a while.'

"'I tink dat sort of funny,' Victoria say, 'an' after a little while I gits out ob de bed and go to the doah—soft-like. An Eva ain' dere.' Victoria she look way outside de doah—real quiet—and here is Eva standin' by a big bush talkin' to somebody. She say she know it was Mistuh Mack talkin' to Eva, 'cause he's de only man dat wears a sailor hat. Dey stan real close and he hug her, but she cain' hear what dey say."

The boys were moving closer to where I stood now, and I decided to enter the barn casually. I said, "Good morning," and followed them as they attached the milking machines.

"I bet you is de firs' one up in yo' house," Eddie said. "Sometimes you beat yo' daddy, eh?"

"I wanted to catch the low tide," I said. "I almost always wake up early. It's nice and cool now." I followed them around the barn. "What's new?" I asked. Such a question often evoked an amorous account of how they had spent the previous evening.

"Nothin' new any mo'," Oscar said, affecting weariness. "Same ole ting. I jus' wuk hard all day an' go to bed, and den get up an' wuk some mo'."

It was clear that neither of them was in the mood for conversation with me, and certainly they were not about to resume talk of Eva and Charlie as long as I stood around.

I sauntered down to the water's edge where I absently worked with the dip net while my thoughts raced around in tight little circles. You did hear something real just now, and a God-awful-lot it was, too. Charlie Mack is in love with a Negro girl! No, he isn't—she was talking to someone else standing there in the bushes. Then my thoughts would go in reverse, and Oscar's story would flash before me like pictures on a screen. Sure—that had to be Charlie Mack standing by the bush; a black man wouldn't hide like that.

One morning at the barn Oscar said to Eddie, not knowing that I had arrived, "Victoria keep telling Eva she got to stop talkin' to Mistuh Mack. 'Jes doan talk to him nowhere!' she say." He turned and saw that I had heard all. He ducked quickly behind a cow to adjust the milking machine. Was he going to pretend that I hadn't heard what he said? The least I could do to save him would be to walk away casually. But suddenly his head reappeared. He looked at me—intently, unsmiling—and said in a low voice, "Clyde, I guess you know all 'bout dis problem. I sure hope you doan talk 'bout it. I doan tink yo' daddy know 'bout dis yet, and I sure hope he doan find out. I doan want Mistuh Charlie and Eva to have no trouble, but it look like dey is sho' headed dat way."

I felt worried about Eva and Charlie, but I also felt good about being on the inside of this story.

"I'll never tell anyone, Oscar. This is a secret between us."

"Dat's good. Somethin' like dis nevah happen on dis Bluff befo'. It jes 'bout drive Victoria and me crazy."

"Do you think they want to get married?"

Oscar let out a sigh. "Victoria 'fraid she sister do some dumb ting—like run away, maybe. Fo' de las' two weeks Eva been going up to Mistuh Mack's house. I can't think o' no worse ting dat gal can do. Las' Sunday night when her daddy and mammy go off to church, she say, 'I tired. I jes doan feel like walkin' so far.' But after it git dark she walk up along de edge of de creek by de gin house, and hug de bank by dat high groun' below Mistuh Mack's house, and go roun' to de back do', and he let her inside. Dat night Victoria walk back from church a little faster dan de res', and see Eva jes sneakin' back into de house. Victoria say, 'I know where you bin, and I gonna tell my mother.' Eva beg her sister not to say nothin' and Victoria say, 'Well, not dis time.' Den las' Sat-dy dat fool gal go again!"

In these conversations I saw a new side of Oscar and Eddie. At other times as they had gone about their work, they had told me lightly and, I suppose, half truthfully of their adventures with girls. They had been my introduction to the boastful talk of young men who mingle fact with fantasy, keeping a sly eye open to note the effect their story produces. This time Oscar and Eddie were not trying to impress me; they were letting me share a concern for other people. Conquest and gratification were repugnant to them now, it seemed, but neither did they give way to censure and blame. Oscar and Eddie had never heard of the concept of classical tragedy, but what they saw skirted close to the classical concept— a man and a woman caught up in powerful forces that lead inexorably to heartbreak and disaster. Their sadness at what they saw made them now talk like the grown-up white men whom I knew, not like two big boys looking for adventure.

I tried to spend more time at the store—the only place where I could observe Charlie and Eva together. Try as I might, I could detect no difference in their demeanor. I was used to seeing Eva come into the store to buy an item for her mother, and I thought nothing of it except that she was prettier and quieter than the other girls. We all thought she was lucky—and deserving—to have the job at Oyster Point; the Ravenels could not have chosen better. Now, I noticed that she came into the store every evening after work, and I began to watch her more closely. She lingered at the counter to talk with Charlie a little longer than she used to, I thought, but not too long. Had she lost her virginity? I wondered what night it might have happened, and if I could tell. I had never been "in" on a secret of this magnitude before and, absorbing as it was, I knew that I would never reveal it to anyone. Eva had obviously told her sister, her sister had told Oscar, and Oscar had told me. Still it was a secret—one that torture on the rack would never draw from me. This was like the Zane Grey novels which I had begun to read—novels that displaced Horatio Alger books forever. Men and women met secretly, kissed passionately, pressed their tense bodies against each other in the dark. I liked to imagine Charlie exploring Eva's body after she crept into his cottage late at night. Had Charlie told anyone of his new love, I wondered. If I were a little older, I liked to think he might share it with me, but I could think of no way to bring up the subject, or to convince him that I deserved his confidence. There was certainly no one else on the plantation to tell, but maybe he talked to friends in the city.

A few days passed before I could again talk with the boys at the barn. Oscar was adjusting a milking machine while I stood back to watch. I felt involved enough now in their problem to ask, "Is Victoria still worried about her sister?" I tried to make it sound offhand.

"Yeah, man, and tings is a lot worse. Night befo' las' her daddy foun' out 'bout Mistuh Mack. He thought Eva was in bed and call to her 'bout somethin'. No answer. Den Victoria have to say, 'She gone out.'

"'Where she gone dis time of night?' Victoria lie; she say she doan know. 'Ax her when she come back,' she say to her daddy. So dey jes gets up and sets dere waitin' for her. 'Bout twelve o'clock Eva come in quiet-like. Dey wasn't no lamps lit, an' jus' as Eva step through de do', her daddy and mammy jump up and say, 'Where you bin?'

"Eva wouldn't say nothin' at firs' an' just stand dere, but her daddy won't give up. He and her mammy yell at her an' say, 'You gonna set in dis chair and tell us where you bin, ef you set dere till mornin'.'

"Eva she cryin' and dey shoutin' at her. Victoria jus' lay dere in de bed and doan say nothin'. After a long time Eva tell dem dat she bin to Mistuh Mack's house. She say he is good to her an' he love her, but dey can't talk to each other no where on dis place. So she go to his house so dey can be alone.

"Her daddy and mammy feel so bad and so worried dey jus' set dere thinkin'. Dey say dey is scared. Dis kind of ting can make so much trouble dey might have to leave de Bluff. 'Where we go den?' dey say. Den her mammy say, 'How come you stay so long wid dat man? You-all ain jus' talk all dat time.' She jump up and grab Eva and say, 'You ain gonna give us a yellow baby, is you?' Eva jus' set dere, still cryin'. 'I doan tink so,' she say.

"'You doan *tink* so!' her mammy scream. 'Oh, Jesus,' she say, 'please take Mistuh Mack back on dat ship and send him away.'

"Eva jump up and say, 'No! If he go, I go wid him.'

" 'Doan talk crazy, gal,' her daddy say. 'You cain go on no ship!'

"Victoria say dey keep talkin' and carryin' on fo' a long time. Den she hear her daddy say, 'I got to talk wid Mistuh Breeze 'bout dis. I doan know when I do it,' he say, 'but I sho' got to talk to dat man.' "

My father had a sweet tooth, my mother used to say, because he ate so much candy. He was so fond of it that once or twice a week he would go into the kitchen after supper, stir two cups of sugar, some cocoa, and milk in a pan and put it on to boil. He would stir with one hand while he read from the *Holstein Fresian World* in the other. One evening he was not reading, but talking to my mother when I walked into the kitchen to check on the candy's progress. Their voices trailed off into nothingness as I approached, and my father turned to testing the candy in cold water. Suddenly he turned and said, "I don't know why you shouldn't hear about this. We've been talking about Charlie Mack. I just found out today that he's been seeing Evalina. I mean she's been going to his house. Her father is awfully upset. It's a dumb thing for Charlie to do—I thought he had more sense."

"Can't her father put a stop to it?" my mother asked.

"He doesn't think he can—now. It's a bad situation."

I remember being surprised by how closely his account squared with Oscar's, although I knew a few more details than my father did. I feigned complete surprise.

My mother, as I had expected, was aghast.

"It just doesn't seem possible!" She was staring absently into the sink.

"I don't think I'd put it that way," my father said. He gave her a droll look. "Impossible? Strikes me it's quite possible."

"We-ll . . . !" My mother drew out the word with a look of pretended outrage. "You know perfectly well what I meant."

My father grinned at her. "You know what I meant, too," he retorted.

But Charlie and Eva's affair was no occasion for levity; it sent my father to Charleston for a long talk with Mr. Lawton who, in turn, called in the Reverend Martin. One could have guessed in advance the outcome of such a discussion. Charlie was, after all, only a temporary worker who had not been promised a career-job on the plantation; he would move on sooner or later, being the restless type, it appeared—sort of a drifter. If a baby should come, it would certainly be better not to have him around. Not that there would be serious trouble—there had been more than one yellow baby born on James Island—but why not reduce the awkwardness to a minimum? Eva's father was one of the plantation's most reliable workers, and he was in obvious distress. His job, he must be told, was not the least in jeopardy, and he should be reassured. The Navy Yard with its high wages, it must be remembered, was making it harder and harder for planters to keep good men. My father was to tell him not to worry. I see now that their discussion was one among men, and about men. It should have hardly have been expected that they would identify with Eva or her mother, though the lives of these women were never to be the same again. Charlie Mack would finish the week, and then move into the Seaman's Home temporarily. It was just too bad, too bad. Charlie could put his name on the list in the hiring hall, and no doubt pick up a ship soon; Charleston harbor was full of traffic in those days. The Reverend Martin would also talk to him, and help work out the transition. It was, indeed, just too bad.

I thought it a little strange that I should be the one who told Charlie of a meeting he was to have with my father and Alison Lawton. But a messenger was needed, since the plantation had no

internal telephone system. I had come to the dairy barn one afternoon, after having just changed my school clothes for everyday
ones, when my father said, "Run down to the store and tell Charlie to stick around a few minutes after closing time. I'll be down
to see him." I thought as I walked to the store, "I've got to make
this sound casual. I won't say that Mr. Lawton is coming, too—
but I'll bet he is." Charlie was putting grits into five-pound bags
as I gave him the message. He asked how school went that day,
and did I really like high school.

"I graduated from high school just four years ago last June." He
had volunteered almost nothing about his personal background,
as I have said, and this little item raised my opinion of him by
several notches. "If I can save up the money, I may go back to
school some day. Sometimes I think I'd like to be a lawyer."

I moved to the doorway for a moment, and saw what I had
expected to see—Eva coming down the creek road to the store on
an errand for her mother. She pushed open the screen door and
entered the room—sweetly poised, as usual.

Hello Mistuh Clyde, hello Mistuh Charlie, hello Eva, hello Eva.
I need some milk biscuits an rice. Can you use five pounds? No,
Mistuh Charlie, dat's too much, 'bout three pounds . . . I returned
to my seat on the oats bin and watched them. How could they
keep it all inside—so calm, so natural? Miz Ravenel say she like
me to bring her two cans of tomatoes an some grits, she send de
money. Mrs. Ravenel is a good customer. You go castin' pretty
soon Mistuh Charlie? Maybe next Friday, Miz Ravenel say she like
some shrimp . . .

Just then I heard Alison Lawton's old Stutz shift gears and turn
up the little grade to the dairy. I jumped off the oats bin. "So long,
Charlie. See you tomorrow. Bye, Eva." I didn't want to hang
around the store any longer.

My father chose to make candy again that evening. We children paid little attention to him during the making of it, although we liked the finished product well enough. His little stay in the kitchen provided the opportunity for my parents to converse while the rest of the family listened to the radio or did homework. I knew that tonight it would be quite permissible for me to go to the kitchen and listen.

"We did a hard thing, today," my father said. "I hope we did right."

"Is Charlie really going to leave us?" my mother asked.

"Oh yes. There's no question about that. Strange, even though he has done something that I suppose is wrong, and . . ."

"You 'suppose,'" my mother interrupted and waited for him to explain himself.

"Yes, I said 'suppose'! I could use the words 'unwise' or 'foolish' a lot easier. But I started out to say, strange how a problem like this—this trouble—causes you to understand a person and to like him a lot more than you ever did before. Mr. Lawton and I hate to see Charlie go. We both think he is basically a very good man. He says Eva is kind and bright and has a heart of gold, and he loves her. He'd take her back to—then he didn't finish the sentence. 'But I can't go home,' he says. 'I guess it would be hard for me to take Eva anywhere. I know now we made a big mistake in letting this thing get started. But she's the kindest, most loving person—the first really that I ever had.'

"Even through all our long talk," my father continued, "we knew Charlie would have to leave the Bluff. We didn't have to decide—we were hunting for an easy way to tell him. But we finally did.

"Mr. Lawton gave him his card on which he wrote my name, too. 'Mr. Mack,' he said, 'don't lose this. Mr. Bresee or I will write you a recommendation whenever you need one. Just let us know.

We want you to get that education and make something of yourself. I wish it could be in this area, but I guess not.' "

"Should I have him up for supper before he goes?" my mother
asked.

"Probably not. There isn't much more for us to say. Why don't
you send him down half a chicken, or something?"

When I came home from school Friday night the store was
closed and Charlie was gone. I stopped at the dairy barn hoping
to find Oscar free for a minute; he was putting meal in front of
each stanchion and was able to talk as he worked.

"Does Victoria tell you anything about Eva?" I asked.

"Yeah. Eva tell her she goin' to de city tomorrow morning on
de early boat."

The early boat was a small launch, always perilously overloaded,
which every Saturday carried fifty or more people and their garden produce to the public market in town. Women stood, unmov-
ing, body-to-body on every square foot of deck space and clung
like insects to the cabin roof. As I fished from the wharf, I used to
watch it go chugging out James Island Creek toward the harbor,
thinking it looked more like a huge floating vegetable basket than
a boat. Eva, Oscar said, was going to gather some collards and
butter beans and get on that boat. He looked at me and shook his
head.

"She ain' even sure where he livin', but Sat-dy she goin' down
to the wharf early. We tell her she cain' jus' walk up to dat sailor
place and ask for Mistuh Mack. Den she say she jus' wait somewhere near de waterfront. But dat gal ain' never goin' to find him."

Late Saturday afternoon the returning launch would disgorge
its passengers at the public wharf a quarter of a mile up the creek
from the store, and women would stream out in all directions to
their homes in nearby plantations; a long straggling line of tired

people would wind through the pasture in front of our house on their way to Stiles Point.

Eva made the trip on the early boat every Saturday that fall, spending the day wandering the East Bay section of Charleston. Oscar, who was now convinced that Charlie had gone to sea, would tell me every Monday morning that she could not find him. Shortly after Christmas he told me that Eva was expecting a baby in the spring, news that startled no one, and that Mrs. Ravenel had told her that she could keep on working until the last month. If Eva confided any of her heartbreak to Victoria and if Victoria told Oscar, the sad little story never reached me. I heard nothing of their last hours together—and I had hoped I would—or of Eva's increasing despair as the winter months passed, or when it was that she abandoned all hope—if she ever did.

Sometime after Christmas we received a letter addressed to The Manager, Bluff Plantation, James Island, South Carolina. The letter, postmarked Baltimore, began with a statement that the writer was the sister of a man named Charlie MacInnes who might have worked on the Lawton plantation. We suddenly found ourselves engulfed again in thoughts of Charlie and Eva. Charlie MacInnes. So that was his name.

Could anyone on the plantation tell the sister where Charlie MacInnes might be? He had left Baltimore four years ago and had been traced to a big plantation near Charleston called the Bluff. The circumstances under which he left home, the sister continued, were unpleasant and she would not go into them, but she would like him to have the message that things were different now, and to please come home. If he could not come, to write. The letter was signed Madeline MacInnes.

We did little that evening but sit around the table and finger the letter which was spread out before us—remembering and speculating.

My father wrote that Charlie had worked here for a few months, that he did a good job, and that he left suddenly. The Reverend Martin had told us that he had shipped out on a freighter registered in Norway, headed for stops at several European ports; since it was a tramp steamer, it might never return to Charleston. No letter had come from him, we were sorry to say, but we would notify her immediately if we learned of his whereabouts. We liked Charlie a great deal, and we hoped there would be a happy homecoming soon.

My mother slowly placed the letter from Baltimore back in its envelope. "Isn't it too bad," she said, "that we can't let Eva have this letter. It might help her a little to know that his family are looking for him, too."

"I suppose it would be kind of nice if she could have it," my father said. Then, as an afterthought: "But I'm afraid she couldn't read it."

A few years ago I returned to James Island to retrace old paths and look up old friends. My father, then aging, had asked me to try to find some of the boys who had worked in the dairy, Oscar, Eddie, Gillie who milked the test cows, Sam Davis, and Cain Aiken, the foreman.

I found only Oscar, retired now and living in one of the neat two-bedroom brick cottages that public housing had made available. His daughter, who looked after him from next door, broke into a big smile when I told her that I had known Oscar when he worked on the Bluff. "He will be so glad to see you. He loved those days on the Bluff." We started walking toward his garden. "I don't know whether those times were as good as he remembers— they seem to get better each year."

Oscar was hoeing a row of young okra plants as we approached him. He leaned on his hoe and nodded invitingly.

"You are Oscar Middleton, aren't you?" I said. "I knew you on the Bluff over forty years ago—but you may not remember me." We shook hands as he searched my face.

"I'll help you out a bit," I said. "My father managed the Lawton plantation a long while ago, and then we moved back to Pennsylvania."

The light of recognition on his face made my thousand-mile trip worthwhile.

"You is Mr. Brezee's son—you is Clyde!" He shook my hand again. I almost hugged him. No more the lean, athletic youth in front of me, but there was the same quick smile; the laughter that seemed to lie just behind his words was still there.

"Please come inside, Mistuh Clyde, where we can sit down an' have a long talk."

"Just a minute, Mr. Middleton," I said. "I was Clyde forty years ago and I'm Clyde now."

"Okay, okay, Clyde." He grinned. "I try."

I told him of my father's wish to hear his voice again, and placed a recorder between us. Would he mind? Anything Mistuh Brezee wanted was fine with him.

For the next hour we tried in a jumbled and disjointed fashion to tell what the intervening years had done to us. He did marry Victoria, they had stayed on the Bluff awhile, and then he had gotten a job with the highway department. Real estate developers were consuming the plantations nearest the city—the Lawton plantation came first—causing unskilled workers such as Oscar to take lands on the far side of the island. Victoria had died two years ago; there were children and grandchildren. As we slowly exhausted the reminiscences, longer and longer pauses began to appear in our conversation. So many of the people that I had known, Gillie Scott, Cain Aiken, Bill Davis, my mother, my brother and sister had died that we almost hesitated to bring up old names.

"Victoria had a sister, Eva," I said. "Whatever became of her?"

"Eva gone now, Mistuh Clyde. She die maybe ten years ago."

I reminded him again that it was Clyde, not Mr. Clyde. "Those days are gone forever, Oscar, we hope."

"Das right, das right," he said nodding slowly. Then quietly, "Dey's almost gone." He was right, of course.

"I've often wondered what happened to Eva," I said, deliberately drawing the conversation back to her. "She liked that young fellow who worked in the store. Do you remember him?"

"Sho' I 'member him. Dat was a long time ago, but I never forget him. Yo' daddy told him he had to leave de place and he went back to town and caught a ship for somewhere. Tings on dis plantation was sure mixed up den. He was a good man but bes' to have him go. Eva never get over dat whole business. Dat girl really grieve. If she had know where he go up North, I tink she would pick up an' left dis island in a minute. But she never fine out. 'Bout five or six years pass, and den she marry a man from Sol Legare way. He a good man."

"Did she have the baby?"

"Yeah. Her mammy and daddy adopt him. You know—dat white boy send Eva money after de baby come? 'Bout every month a letter come wid ten dollars in it, but no return address on de envelope. He do dat fo' a long time."

He stopped and looked at me thoughtfully. "Dat boy is a grown-up man now and he work in de city. You know dat big music sto' on Cannon Street? He sells pianos and guit-tars dere. He name is Charlie."

"Oscar, do you remember his father's name?"

"Sho' I do, man. I never forgit dat. Bet you doan remember."

We sat there facing each other intently across the table—eye-to-eye—each hesitating to speak first.

"His name was Charlie Mack," I said.

"Das right—Clyde."

We both smiled.

## 23

# *This Place Could Go Under*

The August heat settled over the low country in earnest, slowing the pace of life, but bringing at the same time good shrimping, good fishing, and a round of late summer picnics. Some of the planters on James Island went to "the mountains" for a few weeks; the young people returned to tell of cool woods and panoramic views—the kind of scenery I remembered from Pennsylvania. We who stayed on James Island immersed ourselves more deeply in the sea-island life—swimming twice daily, a boat trip to the light-house, or a day at the Rockville races.

But there were new and disturbing thoughts. In my twelfth summer it was inevitable, and certainly desirable, that I should have become aware of the economics that undergirded plantation life. This awareness came to me slowly. I had been spared hard physical labor and, except for gathering cucumbers at four cents a bushel in the spring, I had never worked for pay. There had always been enough food, safety, and supportive people. In our house we simply did not talk about money matters in the larger sense. My parents were people of great reserve. They could not share a concern or a feeling easily. They took their parental responsibilities with religious seriousness, and with a certain pride that was destructive of the "share your problems" style of living. Provide for the children, insist upon a standard of order and obedience, and keep your worries to yourself—especially money worries.

"Moderation" had been the keyword in their upbringing, and they continued to apply it in our own family. They had no patience with people who developed exclusive, "thick" social relationships, and then suddenly "weren't speaking to each other." Be friendly and helpful, but "don't bake your bread in their oven," was a frequent admonition in our household. Maintaining a little distance would save a lot of embarrassing backtracking. My parents seemed able to control the impulse to overspend; they never made purchases to impress people. If no great "highs" in either feelings or aspiration were permitted, neither would there be great "lows." I grew up with the perception, therefore, certainly unexpressed at the time, that life just ran itself.

Like all children, I had my own private collection of fears, but they were threatening only on the edges of my existence. They could be dismissed when I got home. I was disturbed by my father's unexplained shifts in mood—when he would go silent and glum for three days—but my mother compensated for that by never going "into the dumps." Then he would recover. School work was not work, and caused me no anxiety. I had a sturdy body that could run and swim and climb with the best, and I had read more books than any of my friends. I awoke early in the morning before the rest of my family and never could persuade anybody to do anything with me before breakfast, such as fishing or shrimping. Now that I was able to manage a boat alone, I was following the tide tables in the newspaper and planning my day accordingly.

I would frequently go to the milking barns early in the morning. While I had no part in the physical labor of milking, I was more and more a participant in the thinking and the problems of the men who ran the dairy. I was increasingly aware that they had a new anxiety. Our cattle had a health problem. There were cows that had tuberculosis, and the effort to eradicate the disease was decimating the herd. We were reduced to purchasing milk from a nearby plantation. Mr. Tucker, the white man who operated the pasteurizer, was an open, voluble person. He had none of my father's reluctance to talk about money problems.

"Man, this whole operation could go under!" was his blunt appraisal one afternoon when I dropped in at the dairy. He was sitting on a bench by the boiler room eating a baked sweet potato which he had just taken from the coals under the grate.

"What do you mean, 'go under'?"

"This plantation runs on milk. We don't sell enough cucumbers, or potatoes, or beans to keep going. Last year I hear we even lost money on the cukes. We just send those truck crops up to New York and take what they decide to pay us. So—we got to make milk."

He stopped to check some readings on the pasteurizer and to stoke the fire under the boiler.

"Well," he continued, "I've got ten acres of land over by the school where I could make a living if I had to." Mr. Tucker had come from upstate to work on the Bluff. He was not in any sense a planter.

"And your Pa has a big farm back in Pennsylvania he could go to," he said, referring to the fact that my father had recently purchased the farm of his father-in-law.

Back to Pennsylvania? Was such an idea being considered?

"When did he tell you this?" I asked.

"He never said exactly when he's going—never said for sure he would. But you know he really misses those hills and having his own place. Where would you rather live?"

"I guess I like both places," I said weakly.

"Your old man's done a great job here with his herd, and someday this place is gonna make a lot of money. But old Saint Jack could sell it tomorrow if he wanted to. Then where'd we be? You know what? Your pa ought to buy this place and make it work."

Buy the Lawton plantation? He must be kidding. This was something to store away in my mind for a few days, and certainly not a topic that I would bring up first.

Besides, there was the High School of Charleston to worry about. The little community school that I had known on James Island, where half the pupils addressed the teacher as "Cousin," was to be replaced by something complex and fearsome. Students back on Johns Island and Edisto had their own little rural high schools, but the James Islanders mounted a bus and traveled to the city. The High School of Charleston prided itself on being a classical high school—Greek was taught, and the valedictory at commencement was delivered in Latin. Rumors of its terrors and difficulties drifted over to us on James Island. Longing and dread played back and forth in our emotions—longing for the prestige and the great leap into maturity that it brought, and dread of its stern teachers and of the lawless underground in the halls. I did not know it then, but an epoch in my life was ending. The new one would begin with a threat that I had never before experienced—a threat to my sense of personal adequacy.

Only white boys could attend the High School of Charleston, and only white students were picked up by the bus on James Island. My sister, entering her second year at the all-girl Memminger High, and I would meet the bus at the schoolyard, brought there by Bessie and the gig. We would drive Bessie into her stall in the row of stables behind the school, tie her securely, give her a farewell pat, and head for the roadside. My brother, a grade behind me, would remain at James Island School until the bus returned in the afternoon. During those first few weeks of September, we who were starting high school dreaded this trip to

Charleston. Beneath the talk and laughter on the bus as it careened over the dirt roads, the anxiety among the boys ran high.

The High School of Charleston, facing Rutledge Avenue and occupying a lot that extended back to Ashley Avenue, was a fairly new building and it was the pride of the city. Three stories high and made of brick, it had two wings of classrooms that reached nearly to the sidewalk; between these wings was a grassy court and the formal entrance—a door flanked by two tall concrete columns. If I had entered by this door, I might have felt differently about the institution than I did; busses from the country stopped at the drab Ashley Avenue entrance in front of the kind of high steel fence one finds around factories and prisons. The interior of the building was quite undistinguished—the usual egg-crate collection of classrooms, an auditorium, and a gymnasium.

To get into the high school building that first week, freshmen from James Island would have to run the gauntlet, or "the line," as we called it. The line consisted of a double row of upper classmen that extended from the sidewalk to the back door of the school. These boys stood facing each other with belts removed, and at the ready. Country boys unloading on Ashley Avenue were considered prized quarry.

On the first day, some of us James Islanders dashed around to the front of the building and escaped our tormentors. Take no comfort in this; the enemy was onto this tactic, and would have a special committee on hand tomorrow to insure proper entry. Through a combination of luck and good management, I never actually ran through the line. But for the first two weeks of school, the frightening possibility cast a pall over my days.

The High School of Charleston seemed to have operated in those days on the assumption that an education should be made as difficult as possible to obtain. There was virtue in suffering, and jumping hurdles eliminated the unfit. In retrospect, I see the teachers smarting from a comparison of their school with a private military academy, three blocks away—a place where "they maintain standards." I can imagine that every staff meeting at the High School of Charleston was followed by a resolve to "toughen up." The nearby military college, The Citadel, with its indifference to humanitarian values—an institution where my more fearsome teachers had studied—must have cast its baleful influence over secondary education in those days. Toughness became a synonym for quality. The system was especially strenuous on country boys not used to large classes, and not yet hardened by the playground ways of the city. As an elimination course, the system worked; scores of boys were dissuaded from even attempting the High School of Charleston, and many, including two of my friends, dropped out after a few weeks.

The Algebra I teacher probably eliminated more freshmen than any other faculty member. A Citadel graduate, he conducted his classes in the manner of a raging drill sergeant, never smiling, and proclaiming daily that most of the class should be "shot at sunrise." I have been a member of no group since then, except in wartime, where the anxiety level was so high. One day a boy behind me punched me in the back and whispered, "Stop yawning! You'll be shot at sunrise!"

Two-twenty brings the day's ordeal to an end. We bind our books with a canvas strap, and race for Ashley Avenue. In a few minutes the James Island bus, half filled with Memminger girls, touches the curb, and we fight our way aboard. Back across the Ashley to trees and quiet roads. In a few minutes we have turned onto the King's Highway, clay surfaced and bordered with hedgerows. We pass black children on foot returning from their school at Cut Bridge. We do not see them; they do not see us. Our bus reaches the James Island schoolyard, now empty. Kenneth waits with Bessie and the gig at the roadside. We squeeze onto the narrow seat, and my brother cracks the reins on Bessie's back. She begins the trip home at a pleasant trot and keeps it up past Crazy Pigeon's house, but soft sand soon brings her down to a heavy walk. We pass Cain Aiken's house on the hill. Cain is the field foreman and has a house with an annex. The road now leads along James Island Creek; Crazy John is at the water's edge as always, searching. We pass Ellen Whaley sitting on the steps of her cabin, smoking a pipe. We call out to her.

"Hello, Ellen. How are you?"

We like Ellen Whaley and she knows it.

"I'se fine, tank you. How you-all?"

"We're O.K., Ellen."

"God bless you chillun real good, now. Tell Miz Breezy howdy, for me."

The dairy boys are moving the cattle into the barns for milking. The geese have corraled themselves around the hay barn for the afternoon handouts. The old exultation is returning. I am back among loved and familiar things. We leave the gig for Ned to take care of. Our father appears from the dairy building. "Well, how did things go today?" I lie, as usual. "O.K. Fine." My pride doesn't let me tell of "the line" we had dreaded, my embarrassing failure on the parallel bars, the terrifying algebra class, the anxious lunch break spent on the third floor. I report that Edgar Allan Poe actually lived on Sullivan's Island, and that I had seen a replica of the Rosetta Stone; things are fine, I am on top, do not worry, the family honor is intact.

Home again—home again. Home to a world that I can manage. This plantation now is mine. The restless cattle, the broad fields, and the men who work them, the streams and inlets, the shabby cabins, the creaking windmill, this pleasant winding down of the day's work—all are mine. They have no power to frighten me. I

feel quiet and strong. I race up the pasture road toward home.
Through the back door and into the kitchen where Azalee is waiting. Although her work for the day is done, she stays to make
peanut butter sandwiches and to talk awhile. She is seventeen,
gentle and bright, surely one of the prettiest girls on the Bluff. She
has none of my worries, for she stopped school after third grade.
She has only to please my mother, who is unfailingly kind to her.
We love her. She and my sister sit at the table for a conversation
that ends in a shower of giggles. I change my clothes and walk
back to the plantation buildings. I see the city of Charleston resting low on the water; it sends soft sounds across the marsh and
pasture lands. They give me a twinge of anxiety that I push aside.
Tomorrow, with all its indignities, is far off. Maybe tomorrow
won't come—ever.

Eddie and Oscar call to me warmly as they amble back and forth
behind the row of cows. They do not break their conversation,
begun long before, about girls. I must listen and catch on as best
I can—like jumping on the running board of a moving car. They
clue me in on the main points. I do not volunteer to help with

their work—the carrying of pails, or feeding, or moving the cows to pasture. They would not know how to respond if I did.

I go down to the gin house by the edge of the creek. The field men have just come in from ploughing, and their mules are at the watering trough, drinking deeply and noisily. The men pull off their harness, the mules shake themselves in a series of giant shivers and trot off to their stalls for food. I watch but do not help. They do not expect me to, and would feel awkward if I offered. I go down to the wharf and struggle heavily with a boat. They do not offer to help me. I do not expect them to.

Supper, and my father twirling the dials of the Atwater-Kent radio. If the A, B, and C batteries are at full strength, he will get WJAX, Jacksonville, where a lady never tires of singing "Florida Nights." Then to my homework; a growing distress mounts inside of me that I can no longer confine to a spot in my stomach; by the time the algebra homework is done, anxiety envelopes me completely. I copy the algebra problems in ink, fold the paper once—and do I place my name on the second or third line? I have forgotten. Oh, God!

There were surely examples of teaching at its worst in the High School of Charleston, but as the months passed, I was to discover men whom I slowly found myself wishing to emulate. John Gibbs sat on the edge of his desk, propped his feet on another, and talked about "literature and life." Charleston certainly had more history than any other place that I had ever heard about, and from John Gibbs I learned that she had an equally large share of writers. His interest ranged widely. There was not the narrow patriotism that I had felt in James Island Grammar School. Some of those Yankees up North could write, too.

He was particularly fond of Sullivan's Island. This historic island, facing the Atlantic Ocean, projected its southern tip to the entrance of Charleston harbor. Here Fort Moultrie was built. John

Gibbs, born and educated in Charleston, no longer had to look up in books the fascinating lore of the low country. I relived the battle with the British when Sgt. Jasper seized the fallen flag and planted it once more "on the summit of the merlon."

The story he told of General Moultrie was great history, and certainly one sentence was great literature. General William Moultrie was taken prisoner by the British on Sullivan's Island at the fall of Charleston. The British sought twice to get him to defect, but failed. He was first offered the restoration of his plantation estate, and payment for all damages he had sustained if he would switch his allegiance. The second offer came from another British general, offering him sanctuary in Jamaica and full return of all his lands if he would abandon his cause. He refused both offers, stating in a letter that he would go on as he had begun, "standing in the defense of liberty." And then comes the great sentence: "You have forgotten to tell me where to hide myself from myself; no simple fee of the valuable island of Jamaica would induce me to part from my integrity." This was, indeed, literature and life.

The young Edgar Allan Poe was also drawn to the wind-swept beaches of Sullivan's Island. John Gibbs liked to talk about Poe.

"Let me read to you the gloomiest opening sentence in American literature: 'During the whole of a dull, dark, and soundless day in the autumn of the year when the clouds hung oppressively low in the heavens . . .' Get out your books and turn to *The Fall of the House of Usher.*" He gave us the page. "Find it and stay with me . . . 'I had been passing alone on horseback, through a singularly dreary tract of country, and at length found myself, as the shades of evening drew on, within view of the melancholy house of Usher.'" I, too, had walked through brown, abandoned fields on noiseless afternoons in autumn, the clouds low in the heavens, and dry broom grass up to my waist. I could see the melancholy house of Usher half buried in a tract of woods we called "thirty-six." I memorized the sentence instantly. As the bus bounced over the James Island roads that afternoon, I found myself muttering, "During the whole of a dull, dark, and soundless day in the autumn of the year . . ."

## 24

# *The Fear That Plagued*

My brother's illness seemed to begin with the Sunday school picnic at Folly Beach. There was no place where the children could have more fun on a summer day than at the newly opened Folly Island beach and pavilion. The Sunday school obtained special admission tickets to the island, and special reserved tables at the lower end of the boardwalk. Our little caravan of cars arrived at eleven o'clock; the mothers tried to make themselves comfortable on wooden benches as they guarded the picnic baskets; and the children played in the surf. Then the dinner, the prescribed one-hour wait, and into the water again.

Kenneth did not feel like swimming in the afternoon, but stretched out on one of the benches, complaining vaguely of stomach pain; he later vomited. No doubt, there were some foods in his stomach that "didn't go together." In those days much was made of wrong combinations: "Milk and fish make my children sick"; "Did he have an orange? Orange and meatloaf are a bad combination"; "It may have been cucumbers and lemonade"; and so on.

He recovered, or appeared to, by evening. But sick spells came every few days, and he became increasingly listless. The next Saturday night when we went to Charleston we called on Dr. Bowers before we went shopping on King Street. He gave Kenneth some medicine, and suggested that he eat easily digested foods.

Later in the summer my brother came down with a cold; he had been sweaty, the explanation went, and he had carelessly slept in front of an open window. A rare, cool breeze had blown on him, and he had awakened feeling chilly. My father, whose growing anxiety I was now beginning to sense, was not impressed by this simple theory and took his temperature. It was elevated, but not alarmingly so for a child.

"I don't like his cough," I heard my father say one evening. "He doesn't act right. I think it's more than 'just a cold.' "

"Well, what do you think?" my mother asked.

"I don't want to think," he said as he walked out of the door and toward the Bluff.

My brother's general symptoms could be the forerunner of a dozen ailments, or perhaps of none; besides, there were days when he was his old self. Just how concerned should one be? He hadn't felt bad in almost two weeks; each spell, it was hoped, would be the last one.

I did not know then the fear that plagued my father, but I should have known; this boy might have tuberculosis, the dread disease that could attack any organ, including the bones. Tuberculosis was on the mind of everyone in those days, but because of the anxiety it evoked, the word was rarely on anyone's tongue.

The "colds" that Kenneth had did not produce racking coughs, but they were annoying; if he needed to expectorate during the night there were squares of folded tissue under his pillow. If used, they were tossed on the floor. Now my father always awakened early in order to be at the barn during the milking; it was unthinkable that he should not be there for this daily observation of the cows, one by one. I, too, was a natural early riser, and I would often hear his footsteps approach our bedroom door, though I sometimes feigned sleep. He always looked in upon us before he went downstairs.

One morning I was awake when he came to the door, although I kept my eyes closed. This time he stood at the door a moment, then walked to Kenneth's side of the bed and picked up one of the discarded squares of paper. He examined it, and then another. As he stood there I heard something I had never heard before. My father was crying. I feigned sleep as I never had before; he left the room, still sobbing softly. I got out of bed and looked at the crumpled tissues. They were red. My brother was coughing blood. I knew then why my father wept; I had not studied "Health and Hygiene" in James Island Grammar School for nothing. This was the critical symptom—the symptom that meant tuberculosis of the lungs. True, I had read that a case of pneumonia could cause a pink expectorate, but he did not have pneumonia—or a throat infection—and he did not have a sore throat.

My father came up for breakfast that morning, silent and red-eyed, but he did not cry again. A telephone appeal was made to Dr. Bowers. Yes, he would come over this evening and bring two specialists, a lung-and-heart man and an internist. Kenneth should stay in bed today and drink lots of liquids. My mother thought it best to open both windows in his room.

Later in the forenoon I went down to the Bluff hoping to find Jamsie. In a few minutes I saw him coming down the creek road and we met at the wharf.

"Want to fish?" I asked him.

"Yeah, but we ain't got no bait."

Luckily, the tide was right and we put down a couple of dip nets. Shrimp are plentiful in August, and we soon had a couple dozen of them jumping around on the wharf.

"Let's stay here and fish," I suggested. Jamsie was agreeable and we threw out our lines.

"I heah dat yo' brother is pretty sick," Jamsie said. How had he heard so soon, I wondered. I asked him.

"Dey tell me when I was at de sto'."

Well, of course, why not? Anyone at the store would know because the telephone was there.

"Mistuh Knight tink he pretty sick. He say he never seen yo' daddy feel so bad."

"Yeah," I said. "Kenneth may have TB. That's the disease a lot of the cows have."

After a moment Jamsie said, "I guess he's pretty bad, den."

The three doctors came that evening. They were pleasant, grave men who gave my father their hats and shook his hand. He then led them upstairs, followed by my mother. Gladys and I stayed in the parlor and tried unsuccessfully to make the radio work. Five or six controls had to be adjusted to receive clear sounds, and we could not get the combination right.

After a while my mother came downstairs, her face tense and drawn. To our questioning looks she said, "Your brother is a pretty sick boy."

A little later the doctors came downstairs and conferred with my father in the hall. After they had picked up their hats, the doctors came to the parlor door and said simply, "Good night, Mrs. Bresee," and left.

My father came into the parlor and dropped on the sofa beside my mother. "They give him only a fifty-fifty chance," he said, and covered his face. My mother silently wiped her eyes with the back of her hand; my father wept.

Our parents were not able to tell us in any detail that evening what the doctors had said. Before we slipped off to bed someone mentioned that it would be better if "Clyde sleeps in the little bedroom for a while."

The most advanced curative procedures of the times were begun immediately. First, there must be fresh air. Arthur Brown, the carpenter, was called to screen the east end of the porch, and cut a new door into the dining room. The Lawtons sent an iron single bed that we stood on wooden blocks on the porch. Canvas awnings were installed on the south and east sides of the porch, as well as a canvas curtain that could be drawn around the room to keep out the wind and rain. In a surprisingly short time Kenneth was living on the porch day and night. He was prescribed bed rest and high-protein foods. Juices pressed from fresh beef were recommended for him daily, and I soon found myself forcing a heavy cast-iron press down on a piece of raw beef until I had collected a half cup of the pink fluid.

Months passed while Kenneth read, worked puzzles, and entertained visitors. I even set up my Weeden steam engine by his bed. We did bring him inside for the hurricane in September, when the wind took off the awnings and blew down all the chinaberry trees in the pasture; the next day he was back on the porch.

Slowly he began to recover; there was more strength in his arms and legs, and the color returned to his face. The cough had long since disappeared. Although he had lost a year of school, he was almost himself again the following September.

The doubts and misgivings of my father would only grow stronger. Had Kenneth contracted the disease from our milk, pasteurized though it was? This was a controversial matter. Or were the virulent bacteria lurking everywhere on the plantation? The presence of tubercular animals on the Bluff was now becoming intolerable—for new and terrifying reasons.

# 25

# *Your Formative Years*

Kenneth's convalescence altered greatly my role in the family, as it did that of my sister. Almost overnight we became surrogate parents. I no longer saw him as a playmate or sometime rival, but as my charge and responsibility, on whose recovery I now focused all my efforts. Sick people can and do become burdens, but they can also provide the first brush with adulthood for those who tend them—rallying points, producing in family members, particularly in brothers and sisters, a selfless energy that will match any demand. Such a phenomenon is common, of course, in all strong families, but I had never experienced it until my brother was stricken.

Like all youngsters, I did not know that I was growing up; while "in process" a boy does not know that he is maturing. Even the startling changes of sexual development have to stay with him for a while before they are convincing. Maturation is observable only from the outside and from a distance. He suddenly wants the challenge of a bigger bicycle; old books and games are put aside and "better" ones replace them; dreams and plans that are as natural as breathing seem to spring from nowhere. One is supposed to become an adult through jerks and bumps that the school calls "grade promotions," but like many boys, I did not. My movement did not correspond very well to "grade levels." I experienced spurts of wonder and curiosity and leaps of fancy, and then inexplicable eddies of complacency when I must have lagged alarmingly behind the so-called norms and expectations of my mentors.

Once, long after we had returned to Pennsylvania, a neighbor asked me, "How old were you when you lived on that Southern plantation?"

"I lived there until I was past fourteen."

"You were there for the most formative years of your life, weren't you?" he remarked.

I had never before thought of those years in that light, and I have often wondered since, "What was being formed?" Whatever it was, it happened without my knowing it. Others, perhaps, can state precisely what they observed being formed, but even at this distance I can make only a few tentative generalizations.

I came to the Lawton plantation and to the entire James Island culture as a consumer and observer—as any child would, but it seems to me now that I remained in that state for a surprisingly long time. Being a participant—a doer—came later to me on that Southern plantation than it would have on a Pennsylvania dairy farm. The varied and colorful life on the Bluff fed my appetite for romance and small adventure; a sense of the past, uncommon in children living elsewhere, was planted in me early, and nourished in a thousand small ways by my play and school experience. My Northern neighbor's observation about the formative years carries a hidden error, for people are being continuously formed and also "unformed." The years as a Southerner did not pour me into a mould—there is probably no such thing as an enduring mould, but certainly "a sense of history," whether innate or acquired, was greatly intensified by the James Island experience.

The watcher-spectator role that I played on the plantation did not permit any entrepreneurial impulses. Actually, there were impulses but they were seldom rewarded. There was almost no way for a child to earn spending money. The only pocket money I earned on the Bluff came from a few days of cucumber picking and the sale one summer of four roosters that I had raised in the backyard. We begged our parents for permission to sell Cloverene salve and thereby earn attractive "premiums," as many of our friends at school did. We always got an emphatic "No! It's just another way of begging from house to house." I tried unsuccessfully to get three families to subscribe to the *Youth's Companion* for a premium banjo—which my parents later consented to buy for me—and we sold a few dozen crabs to Mrs. Posey, who I am convinced did not really want them. Any job that approached offering steady pay was out of the question. In those nonmechanized days of farming, Oscar, Eddie, and Gillie did a hundred small tasks that I could easily have performed. But, as always, there was that distance to maintain.

The sense of distance was not lessened by the fact that I spent much of my time with people whom I thought to be my social, intellectual, and economic inferiors. True, there was a degree of compassion—expressed largely in intellectual terms—and much affection, but there was always the distance.

We who grew up on James Island cannot claim to be the product solely of a rural, low-country culture, for in one sense we were suburban Charlestonians, particularly those of us who grew up on the Bluff. As people who live by the ocean are never for a moment free of that which is half of their horizon, so we on the Lawton plantation, rustic and pastoral as it was, were never free for a moment from the Ashley River, the harbor, and the Charleston peninsula. It was not by chance that the modern highway cutting through the Lawton plantation from James Island Creek to the Cuthbert house and beyond was named Harbor View Drive. Charleston became half of my horizon, both socially and intellectually. In addition to shopping trips, movies, music, the Charleston Museum, there was the High School of Charleston, an institution that hastened my growing-up process in a way that I could not then perceive.

In this classical high school I came to know for the first time men who were not associated with agriculture. Theirs was a world of books and ideas and interesting talk and they made a living without planting and harvesting uncertain crops, or trying to keep cows healthy and producing milk. Someone had told me that teachers didn't get rich. But the planters I knew didn't get rich, either. In a bad year I had heard what families ran up huge accounts at Buck's grocery store. It was always the fathers and grandfathers who had made the money. Teachers seemed to know about the things that I wanted to know about; if they didn't know, they had the time and the wherewithal to find out. Finding out things? Was that what I craved? It was great fun to run into new ideas in history class or in John Gibbs's English class. It was fun to tell people things—to startle them a little. The experience I had in church and PTA giving recitations and little speeches were fun. I liked to watch the smiles come over twenty-five faces all at once at something I had said. At high school I was seeing grown-up men doing what I enjoyed doing and getting paid for it. A picture of myself as an adult, doing an important job and earning my living, was beginning to emerge.

But how long would we remain on James Island? I could not forget Mr. Tucker's grim picture of the plantation business and his last remark, "Your old man ought to buy this place and make it work." The thought staggered me and I had not mentioned it even to my brother, though the idea was never out of my mind. Plantations like this were not sold—they were passed on. This had been the Lawtons' land since 1813. Could a man from up North, like my father, break this tradition of family succession to the land? He might, because Alison Lawton had no children. Actually, St. John Alison Lawton had not chosen to be a planter; he had studied architecture at Virginia Military Institute and had hoped to start his own firm in the city. But the land again, and family succession. Cecilia Lawton, ever confident and assertive, had demanded after the death of her husband that the only son and heir return to the family plantation; it had sustained his father and grandfather and it would sustain him. She would establish the Battery Dairy in Charleston and sell milk that Alison would produce on their plantation.

Sometimes I let my thoughts wander—the Bresee plantation, it might be called; another French Huguenot name to be added to the low-country list. Eddie and Oscar and Gillie would work for us now, and not the Lawton Plantation Battery Dairy complex. Some new tractors perhaps and some new barns, but the same fields, the same old house by the live oaks; the peacock would still give its shrill squawk in the evening when the field bell rang; the tides in the inlet would not change. Nothing important would have to change, would it? Couldn't one come back to all this at evening as I was doing now—maybe from teaching a class in the High School of Charleston that didn't scare the kids to death? It could be the best of two worlds.

Someone else would have to decide what to plant, what to buy and sell. The business of agriculture did not hold me—at least, it had not so far. But the plantation did. What held me may have been something of which the plantation was only a tangible symbol. It was here that my awareness of history had first been aroused—where I first sensed how generations came and went on the same soil, moved among the same old landmarks, and even amid all the fluctuations of life found a certain permanence. Fluctuations there had been in that James Island culture, but the elegance had persisted—a fading elegance, to be sure, but I loved it and loved what lay beneath it.

If by some turn of fate my father should buy the Lawton plan-

tation, would ownership of the land work its ageless magic and turn us into planters? I am sure that the process had already begun in my father. As a youth, I could not know that the age of planters was ending; no one on James Island could ever reverse the changes that even then were beginning to occur. I had come just in time to feel the last warmth of fires about to be extinguished—as were the little fires we used to kindle by the rising tidewater in the floodplain behind our house—swept away by forces as strong and inexorable as the very tide itself.

## 26

# Home Hills

I was now beginning to realize more fully that the economic life of the plantation did not run itself. For much of my life plowing, planting, harvesting, and milking had come with the sunrise and sunset. But I now sensed a pervasive anxiety beneath the pastoral simplicity I had always known. The chief source of this anxiety was, of course, tuberculosis.

Although the efforts to eradicate the disease were now moving closer to success, there were alarming ups and downs. Now, only one or two diseased cows would be found; at the next testing there would be a half-dozen reactors.

My father's diagnostic skill in locating diseased cows that the tuberculin test had missed was, in fact, a bitter success. One dark day after the decision had been made to achieve an accredited herd at any cost, twenty-one animals were marked for destruction. Butchers in Charleston were notified to come over and make their bids. The next morning the cows were kept in their stanchions after milking; trucks backed up to the barn. My father moved down the line of cows, indicating the ones that were to go. "This one . . . and this one . . . and . . ." He put a colored mark on each doomed animal. They were taken to the city abattoir where the veterinarian supervised the slaughter, saving those parts of the carcasses that were fit for human consumption. Expensive, high-producing cows were sold at "bologna prices."

The milking that night was gloomy business. There was less crowding and pushing as the cows came into the barn from pasture. The dairy boys went steadily about their work, but they had no interest in talking. As my father came into the barn, he found Eddie standing absently beside his milking machine. He shook his head slowly. "Man, seems like I don't even see dese cows. I just see de empty places."

What my father and Eddie did not know on that dark afternoon was that the herd had "turned the corner." The next test six months later would find the herd "clean"—and so would the next one.

The possibility of owning the plantation was coming more and more into the open. Such a move was not a round-table topic of conversation in the Bresee family, but from bits of talk I knew that Mr. Tucker's solution was at last receiving serious thought. Mr. Lawton would be willing to sell; that point seemed to have been established. I was not to know until years later, when I had read Mr. Lawton's early letter to my father, that he had indeed envisioned my father as eventually owning the plantation. The decision to seek an accredited herd—agreed upon by both men—would mean a costly interim of several more years with the ultimate reward to come later. But how much later? And to whom? A share of the plantation's profits for my father had been a key inducement in Alison Lawton's offer to have us come to James Island.

If tuberculosis were permanently eradicated and the herd could be advertised as accredited, then the plantation could sell at a handsome profit the blooded young stock that my father knew so well how to produce. Moreover, he envisioned modern methods of marketing liquid milk—methods quite incompatible with the antiquated ones of the Battery Dairy. Alison Lawton was not a young man, and he had no immediate heirs. There must be profound changes, and if my father would reap the harvest for enduring the lean years, it was clear that he must own the plantation.

Willie Mikell of Stiles Point, a man whose land adjoined ours to the east and whom my father greatly respected, drove over to our house early one evening, and the two had a long conversation under the oak trees. I never heard the details of their talk, but apparently my father found fresh support for proceeding with his plan to seek financial aid from a well-to-do cousin in buying the plantation.

Those below-the-surface negotiations made scarcely a ripple in my activities, until the day the telegram came. It had been telephoned from the city to the store just before my father came home to supper. He read it aloud to us. Our New York state cousins Frank and Cora would like to pay us a visit next week. I had met them at the Bresee family reunion the previous summer, and we had stayed an evening in their home. Obviously, they were rich. Cousin Frank had established a large department store in an upstate city, which he had now turned over to his four sons. Yes, he would like to look over the plantation and they would stay until Saturday, if that was agreeable with us.

Now it was, indeed, all on the table—our dining room table to be specific, with five people sitting around it. No more guessing about what was going on: Cousin Frank was considering—this word was emphasized—lending us enough money to buy the Bluff. We mobilized for action. First, sleeping arrangements: the guests would have the bedroom upstairs that faced west, Gladys would take the little room, and Kenneth and I would double up. Azalee would be asked to work overtime to help with the evening meal.

"You boys will clean all the fireplaces and tidy up the yard—tomorrow morning! And can't Ned or somebody fix that hinge on the front gate?" My mother was making notes on a pad as she talked.

"We ought to have fish at least once. I don't think we'd better risk shrimp or crabs. Can Jamsie get us some flounders? I wish Uncle Peter were still here."

"We've got a couple of chickens that aren't laying," I volunteered. "Let's give 'em chicken once."

"O.K.," my mother said and wrote down "chicken." "And you," she was looking at my father, "must get those two posts for the table that you always promised. We'll have to make it long, and I won't have their plates jumping up and down while they eat."

Our dining room table was an oval one with only a central support. When the table was stretched to its full size, a person cutting meat at one end could cause the other end to bob up and down. My father had promised for several years to put in a couple of supports, but had never done so.

"I never saw any plates jumping around in all the years we have lived here," my father observed.

"Well, they do, and it embarrasses me to death." My mother gave him a long, serious stare. "If you want to make a good impression on your cousins, here's your chance."

I discovered the next day that there was also a flurry of activity down at the Bluff—cleaning the barns, cutting weeds, brushing the cows.

We children were at school during much of the three-day visit, but from what I saw, it had been a social success. What Cousin Frank thought of the plantation as an investment possibility was less clear. He must have experienced some of the same shock that we had felt upon our first arrival at the lack of pretentiousness of the buildings. His idea of a farm was colored, no doubt, by his upstate New York background. There the showpiece of a farm was a large, three-storied barn—trim and tight—built to withstand the

Northern winters. The sprawling, simply constructed pens, sheds, and cow barns doubtless gave him pause. The cluster of shabby cabins for the hands, the barefooted, ill-clad Negroes he passed on the roads could not have strengthened the investment impulses of the owner of a large department store. As for historic buildings like the Cuthbert house, ancient trees, and the Old World skyline across the Ashley, these could hardly yield firm returns on his money. Three-quarters of a mile of waterfront directly across from Charleston probably did not mean as much to him as it did to us.

But he and his wife also saw certain beauties in the low country. After an early supper one evening, my father said, "Let's walk down to the James Island Creek. I think the tide is in tonight." I'm sure he knew that the tide would be at its full height, for flood tide on the Bluff at sunset would be a picture our guests would always remember.

We walked through the grove of live oaks and down the path to the plantation buildings. We gazed at the Charleston skyline across the pasture at our right. We went by the silent dairy barns and down to the store and the wharf. I did not then perceive the contrasts in the scene, but they were surely present, and our cousins must have noticed them. A water oak—so large and low and spreading that I could walk upright into its branches—sheltering the store. The store itself, with its blinds closed for the night, its clapboard sides weatherbeaten and whitewash peeling. Ned and his wife sitting on their cabin steps at the edge of the Negro settlement, smoking and watching us. A rowboat pulled up on the shore giving off the odor of a rotting fish that was floating in the leak-water. The inland sea before us, and the setting sun to the west.

We moved to the end of the wharf and became silent. Standing on the rough planks, with the water busy around the piles a few inches below our feet, we gazed out upon a mile of flooded marshland. A vast lake, pink in the sunset light, and broken here and there by patches of reed grass barely showing above the surface, stretched to a far-off line of trees. We watched as the sun turned a deeper and deeper red and slipped out of sight behind the distant woods.

My cousin, speaking half to himself and half aloud, said, "Well, well, well. This is the Carolina low country." Turning to his wife, he commented, "We're a long way from New York state, aren't we, Cora?"

A great blue heron in the marsh grass beside us lifted himself on his long legs, slowly unfolded his wings, and flapped casually off into the western sky. We watched his form disappear in the half-light, and then as the tide turned and began its sweep back into Charleston harbor, we started home.

On another day, we asked our neighbor and expert boatman, Tom Welch, to take our relatives on a short cruise in Charleston harbor. One evening Mr. and Mrs. Alison Lawton entertained my parents and the Northern cousins at Charleston's most fashionable restaurant, The Villa Marguerita, on South Battery. My parents came home that night to tell us that the tables were set around an indoor pool on which floated a real gondola. Our cousin visited the Navy Yard and the phosphate plant, and talked to bankers. He would return North to consider the matter.

There was a month of silence and then a letter came early in November, 1929. It began

Dear Cousin,

As you have probably surmised, the recent disaster on Wall Street has radically altered the financial picture for me. It would therefore be quite impossible at the present time for me to consider . . .

The letter produced a mixture of disappointment, resignation and relief. Back in Pennsylvania there would be a kind of security.

The large farm that my father had bought from my mother's parents could, with much effort, be put into production. Falling milk prices, shaky banks, the drain of the accrediting process, and possibly a longing for a freedom he could not enjoy as Alison Lawton's manager, made the family farm look attractive again. The aging Mr. Lawton, disappointed in the profits from the plantation and frightened by the general economy, would no doubt look for another buyer. Could not other modes of financing be found? I am not sure how much of a risk-taker my father was, and Charleston banks then had few funds to take risks with. The Pennsylvania hills were calling.

New Year's Day morning was uncommonly warm and sunny; I took a bath without using the electric heater. After dinner my brother and I helped my father photograph young calves. For purebred Holsteins to be registered, the owner must supply a photograph or drawing of the animal to accompany the registration papers. In previous years we had held the calves while my father sketched in the markings with a pencil; today we would go modern and use a camera.

"How would you like to do this on our own farm in Pennsylvania someday?"

"I guess it would be nice."

"It would be a lot different from James Island. We'd have our own cows and horses—no mules—and probably a big flock of chickens. You kids could just about take care of the chickens yourselves."

"Then are we really going to move?"

"It looks like the first of March now. We have to get up there before the spring planting."

"Is this still a secret, or can we tell?"

"It's no secret any longer."

We children told the news to almost everyone, and found ourselves almost enjoying the astonishment that it produced.

"We're going back to Pennsylvania in a couple of months."

"You mean for a visit?"

"No, for keeps."

"Won't you be back next summer—ever?"

"No. We're going to live there. But you could always come to visit us."

We had made a difference in the lives of a few people. Callers were more frequent, and there were more invitations to supper and tea. We children received more invitations to spend the weekend at other plantations. My spirits alternately soared and drooped. A big farm of our own, those wooded hills, a winter snowstorm, the cousins I liked and wanted to know better. But how can I say good-bye to the kids in our bunch, to all the people on the plantation, to this old house? The people at church seemed almost sad. Azalee said she felt awful.

Mrs. King of Stono plantation, mother of three grown sons, "Cousin Mary Leize" to all the young people of the church, was my Sunday school teacher. After class on the last Sunday we spent on James Island, she called me aside. She had a New Testament in her hands.

"I want you to have this to remember us by," she said. "We can hardly stand the idea of you all going back to Pennsylvania and just dropping out of our lives here. You'll just be caught up in all the business of getting settled, a new school, and I'm afraid you will forget your old James Island friends."

She smiled and gave my hand a little pat. She was a short lady and I now stood six inches above her.

"And," she continued, "I've written some things in the flyleaf and marked some places for you to read, especially. When you find time, I know you will."

As we rode home from church, I sat in the back seat and turned the pages. The text was marked in many places, and inside the cover—"My Wish for You—Numbers 6:24–26"; "My Request for You—2 Timothy 2:15," and a dozen more goals, challenges, prayers.

I fingered the pages wonderingly. Did I really thank her enough? We had all been in such a hurry. I feared that I hadn't. She had spent hours on this—and all for me. I felt a strange new sense of personal worth. I must measure up to all this trust. I resolved to try. Cousin Mary Leize had accomplished her purpose, but neither of us knew it then.

I had kept putting off telling Gertrude Cappelmann. She still had immense faith in me, and now, in my early teens, I had left behind some of my childish ways. I did not tell her until a week before we left, and it turned out to have been unkind. She looked almost dazed and said nothing for a few moments, and then, "I had somehow thought you'd be here—and keep on studying in the city—maybe attend the College of Charleston."

She was having difficulty speaking and a wave of new affection and respect came over me.

"If you must go, you must go. I'm sure it's been a big decision for your parents."

She paused again. "You will have your music wherever you go. It will grow and grow in you for the rest of your life."

She drew a little breath—as if she had finally adjusted to the news I had brought her—and said, "I suppose there are more opportunities in the big state."

Then we became more businesslike. I would see her again next Saturday. She sent her best wishes to my parents.

The warm glow that I had experienced as people said they loved us, would miss us, would write long letters, would come up North to see us was suddenly dispelled one morning when I woke up to the sound of falling boards—Ned was unloading lumber on the front lawn. I felt sick. This lumber was to make shipping crates for our furniture. This was for keeps. As we left for school, the father-son team of Arthur Brown, Sr., and Arthur Brown, Jr., the best carpenters on James Island set up their sawhorses on the grass.

When we returned that afternoon, three bureaus, the sideboard, and some chairs stood on the porch, crated and ready to go.

"What are the barrels for?"

"Dishes. We'll pack them in sawdust."

"How are we going to take the piano?"

"They'll make a big box for it. If you want to take any of your old toys, we'll see if we can put them in with the dishes. Start picking them out, but I'm not sure about room."

It was late afternoon. The house had been emptied of its belongings and we would spend our last night on James Island at the Stono plantation. We walked for the last time through the empty rooms, picking up stray objects, our feet clattering eerily on the bare floors. My father was in the car urging us to hurry.

I had almost reached the car when I stopped and called out, "Wait a minute. I forgot something." I rushed back upstairs and into my room. I had an overpowering desire to be alone—for only a moment—for one last look. There was the marshy inlet below the house, the tide, the low country in microcosm, where I first played with moving water and became intimate with crabs and shrimp and shore birds. There was the city lying low on the peninsula, sending its soft hum across the water; a freighter in the harbor. The late afternoon sun shone on the whitecaps of the Ashley River, on the white superstructure of the freighter, and glinted from the steeples of St. Michael's and St. Philip's. I leaned on the windowsill with my chin in my hands, looking and remembering—resolutely trying to fix this scene in my memory.

A horn sounded below. I turned and bounded down the stairs,

two steps at a time. I climbed silently into the car, pulled the door shut, and waited for my father to start the engine. After a minute my brother asked, "What's the matter? Did you lose something?"

"Yes," I said. "But never mind."